YORK NOTES

JULIUS CAESAR

WILLIAM SHAKESPEARE

NOTES BY MARTIN WALKER

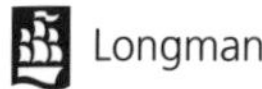
Longman

York Press

YORK PRESS
322 Old Brompton Road, London SW5 9JH

PEARSON EDUCATION LIMITED
Edinburgh Gate, Harlow,
Essex CM20 2JE, United Kingdom
Associated companies, branches and representatives throughout the world

First published 1998
This new and fully revised edition first published 2003
Fifth impression 2007

ISBN-13: 978-0-582-77269-4

Designed by Michelle Cannatella
Illustrations by Judy Stevens
Typeset by Pantek Arts Ltd, Maidstone, Kent
Produced by Pearson Education Asia Limited, Hong Kong

Contents

Part One
Introduction

Part Two
Summaries

Part Three
Commentary

Part Four
Resources

PREFACE

York Notes are designed to give you a broader perspective on works of literature studied at GCSE and equivalent levels. With examination requirements changing in the twenty-first century, we have made a number of significant changes to this new series. We continue to help students to reach their own interpretations of the text but York Notes now have important extra-value new features.

You will discover that York Notes are genuinely interactive. The new **Checkpoint** features make sure that you can test your knowledge and broaden your understanding. You will also be directed to excellent websites, books and films where you can follow up ideas for yourself.

The **Resources** section has been updated and an entirely new section has been devoted to how to improve your grade. Careful reading and application of the principles laid out in the Resources section guarantee improved performance.

The **Detailed summaries** include an easy-to-follow skeleton structure of the story-line, while the section on **Language and style** has been extended to offer an in-depth discussion of the writer's techniques.

The Contents page shows the structure of this study guide. However, there is no need to read from the beginning to the end as you would with a novel, play or poem. Use the Notes in the way that suits you. Our aim is to help you with your understanding of the work, not to dictate how you should learn.

Our authors are practising English teachers and examiners who have used their experience to offer a whole range of **Examiner's secrets** – useful hints to encourage exam success.

The General Editor of this series is John Polley, Senior GCSE Examiner and former Head of English at Harrow Way Community School, Andover.

The author of these Notes is Martin Walker, who is a writer, lecturer and English teacher. He has worked for many years at senior examiner level for an English examination board.

The text used in these Notes is the Longman Literature Shakespeare, edited by Jacqueline Fisher (1992).

INTRODUCTION

HOW TO STUDY A PLAY

Though it may seem obvious, remember that a play is written to be performed before an audience. Ideally, you should see the play live on stage. A film or video recording is next best, though neither can capture the enjoyment of being in a theatre and realising that your reactions are part of the performance.

There are six aspects of a play:

1. THE PLOT: a play is a story whose events are carefully organised by the playwright in order to show how a situation can be worked out
2. THE CHARACTERS: these are the people who have to face this situation. Since they are human they can be good or bad, clever or stupid, likeable or detestable, etc. They may change too!
3. THE THEMES: these are the underlying messages of the play, e.g. jealousy can cause the worst of crimes; ambition can bring the mightiest low
4. THE SETTING: this concerns the time and place that the author has chosen for the play
5. THE LANGUAGE: the writer uses a certain style of expression to convey the characters and ideas
6. STAGING AND PERFORMANCE: the type of stage, the lighting, the sound effects, the costumes, the acting styles and delivery must all be decided

Work out the choices the dramatist has made in the first four areas, and consider how a director might balance these choices to create a live performance.

The purpose of these York Notes is to help you understand what the play is about and to enable you to make your own interpretation. Do not expect the study of a play to be neat and easy: plays are chosen for examination purposes, not written for them!

Be prepared to comment on each of these aspects of the play.

AUTHOR – LIFE AND WORKS

1564 William Shakespeare is baptised on 26 April in Stratford-on-Avon, Warwickshire

1582 Marries Anne Hathaway

1583 Birth of daughter, Susanna,

1585 Birth of twins, Hamnet and Judith

1590–3 Early published works and poems written when theatres are closed by the Plague

1594 Joins Lord Chamberlain's Men (from 1603 named the King's Men) as actor and playwright

1595–9 Writes the history plays and comedies, including *Henry V*

1597 Shakespeare buys New Place, the second biggest house in Stratford

1599 Moves to newly-opened Globe Theatre, *Julius Caesar* probably written

1599–1608 Writes his greatest plays, including *Macbeth*, *King Lear* and *Hamlet*.

1608–13 Takes over the lease of Blackfriars Theatre and writes final plays, the romances, ending with *The Tempest*

1609 Shakespeare's sonnets published

1613 Globe Theatre burns down 29 June, during performance of Henry VIII

1616 Shakespeare dies, 23 April, and is buried in Stratford

1623 First Folio of Shakespeare's plays published

CONTEXT

1558 Elizabeth I becomes Queen of England

1568 Mary Queen of Scots is imprisoned for life

1577–80 Sir Francis Drake becomes the first to circumnavigate the world

1587 Mary Queen of Scots is executed

1588 Defeat of the Spanish Armada

1591 Tea is first drunk in England

1593–4 Outbreak of the Plague in London, closing theatres and killing as many as 5,000, according to some sources

1594 Queen Elizabeth spends Christmas at Greenwich and is entertained by leading theatre company of her day, headed by James Burbage, William Kempe and Shakespeare

1595 Walter Raleigh sails to Guiana

1599 Oliver Cromwell is born

1603 Elizabeth I dies on 24 March; James I, son of Mary, succeeds to throne of England

1604 Peace treaty signed with Spain

1605 The Gunpowder Plot

1611 The Bible is translated into the Authorised (King James) Version

1614 Fire sweeps through Stratford but New Place is spared

1618 Thirty Years War begins

SETTING AND BACKGROUND

GAIUS JULIUS CAESAR (100–44BC)

Caesar was born of a patrician (noble) family, ensuring him wealth and status. He forged a career as a soldier and statesman and, in 60BC, with two other patricians, Pompey and Crassus, formed the first Triumvirate. The three men shared power in Rome. Caesar deliberately sought to please the plebians (the ordinary people) and thus made enemies among the older aristocratic families.

He married three times: Cinna's daughter, Cornelia, in 84BC, Pompeia in 68BC (divorced in 62BC) and Calpurnia in 59BC.

Caesar's power and popularity increased as a result of his successful military campaigns. He conquered Gaul (approximately modern France) between 58BC and 50BC and landed in Britain in 55BC. The loyalty of his armies was directly to him rather than to the government, so making him more enemies among the old noble families, who feared his increasing power.

The death of Crassus in 53BC ended the Triumvirate and for the next few years Pompey allied himself with the Senate (the ruling council), while Caesar maintained control of a large army. Good relations between Pompey and Caesar had, until this time, been maintained by the fact that Pompey was married to Caesar's daughter, Julia.

The Senate was concerned by the popularity and military independence of Caesar and in 50BC asked Caesar to relinquish command of his armies. He refused, and in 49BC led his legions across the River Rubicon (then the northern frontier of Italy), thus initiating civil war.

Pompey fought against Caesar but was defeated by him at Pharsalus, in Greece, in 48BC. Pompey fled to Egypt but was later murdered by the Egyptians. Caesar spent the following winter in Alexandria with Cleopatra, by whom he is said to have had a son, Caesarion. He defeated the remnants of Pompey's supporters in the battles of Thapsus (46BC) and Munda (45BC) and then returned to

CHECK THE NET

Log on to the Shakespeare Birthplace Trust (**www.shakespeare.org.uk**) and see Shakespeare's baptism and marriage entries and his signature.

DID YOU KNOW?

The men of patrician families had ruled Rome before the Republic was founded in 510BC.

DID YOU KNOW?

'To cross the Rubicon' has become a **figure of speech** meaning 'to take a drastic and irreversible step'.

DID YOU KNOW?

Two Consuls, powerful magistrates, held supreme civil and military power in Rome.

Rome, finding it in a state of civil unrest. Caesar was elected Consul and the Senate made him Dictator in order to suppress the riots. Mark Antony was made commander of the cavalry.

Caesar introduced sweeping reforms to the government of Rome. He increased the number of senators to nine hundred by bringing in new members from the provinces and the army. This meant that the senators from the old families were outnumbered. He also assumed the power to declare war; previously only the Senate could do this.

DID YOU KNOW?

The Tarquin dynasty ruled Rome from 753BC to 510BC.

These reforms angered the old families of Rome who saw their long-held power being eroded. Caesar even minted coins bearing his head and appointed his own officials. He then demanded the right to call himself King, when away from Rome, in order to impress his enemies. Kings had been hated in Rome since the days of the Tarquins.

Some of the senators feared Caesar's ambition, thinking that he was going to proclaim himself Emperor. They favoured a republican government, with the Senate holding power. Caesar was assassinated on the steps of the Senate on the Ides of March (15 March) 44BC by a group of Republicans including Brutus and Cassius, on the very day that he was to accept the crown.

CHARACTER TREE

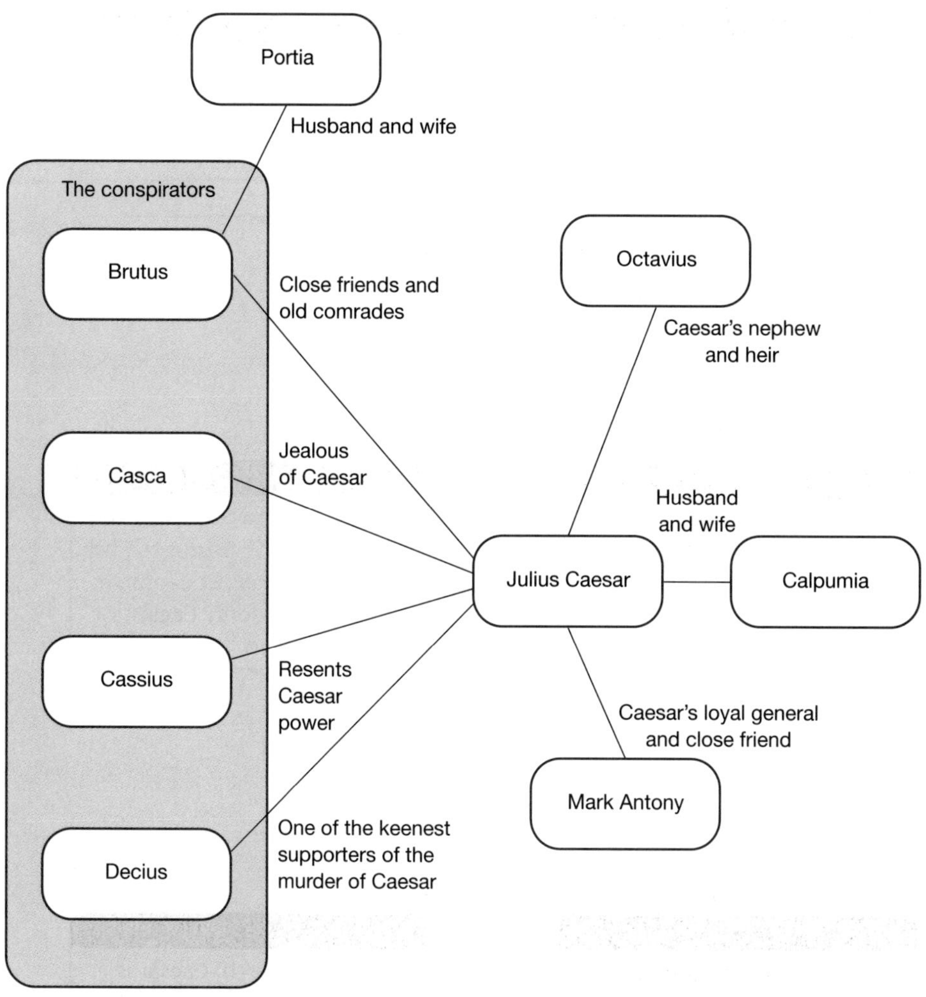

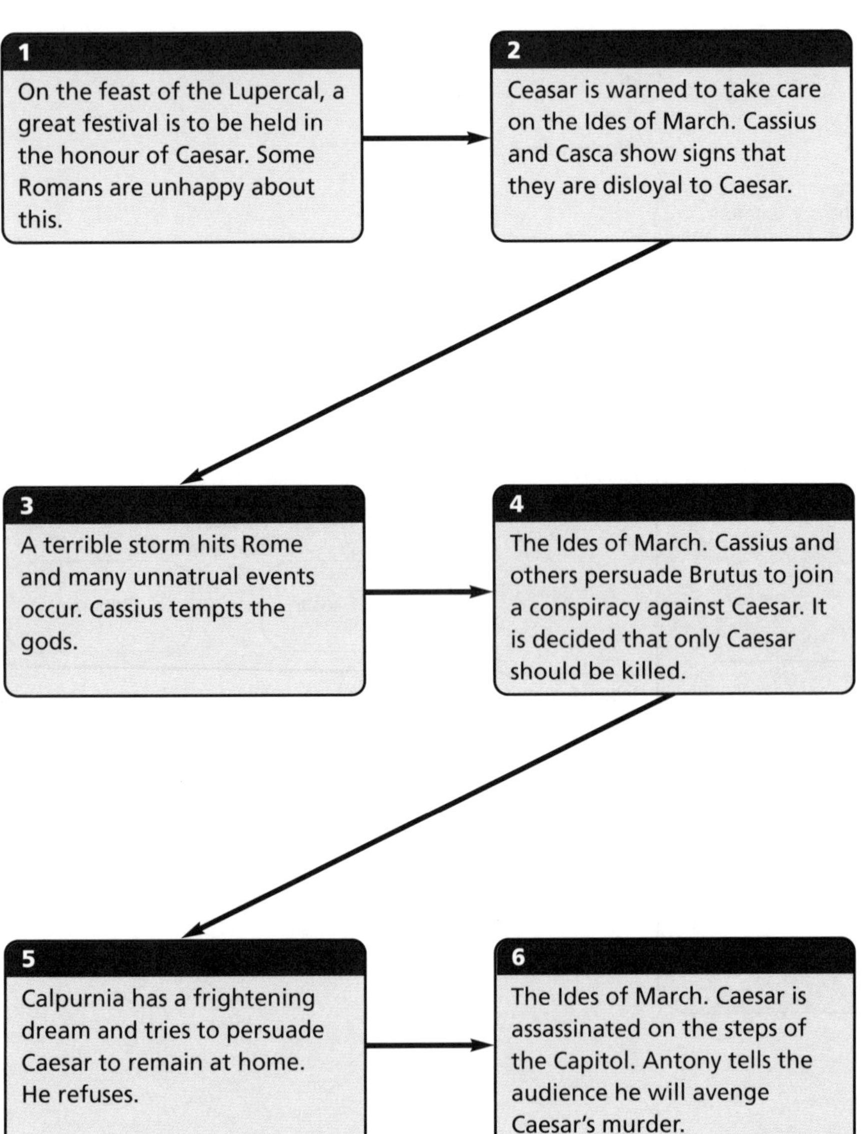
1
On the feast of the Lupercal, a great festival is to be held in the honour of Caesar. Some Romans are unhappy about this.
2
Ceasar is warned to take care on the Ides of March. Cassius and Casca show signs that they are disloyal to Caesar.
3
A terrible storm hits Rome and many unnatrual events occur. Cassius tempts the gods.
4
The Ides of March. Cassius and others persuade Brutus to join a conspiracy against Caesar. It is decided that only Caesar should be killed.
5
Calpurnia has a frightening dream and tries to persuade Caesar to remain at home. He refuses.
6
The Ides of March. Caesar is assassinated on the steps of the Capitol. Antony tells the audience he will avenge Caesar's murder.

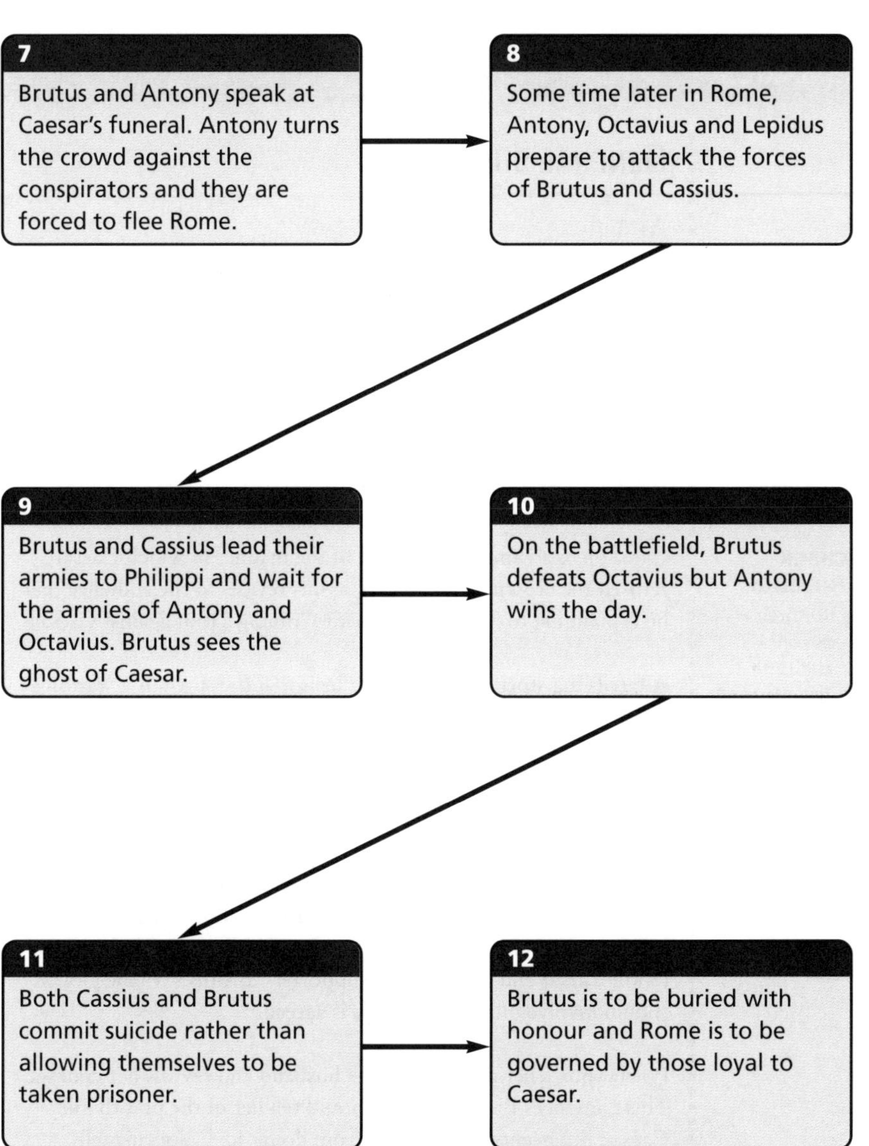
7
Brutus and Antony speak at Caesar's funeral. Antony turns the crowd against the conspirators and they are forced to flee Rome.
8
Some time later in Rome, Antony, Octavius and Lepidus prepare to attack the forces of Brutus and Cassius.
9
Brutus and Cassius lead their armies to Philippi and wait for the armies of Antony and Octavius. Brutus sees the ghost of Caesar.
10
On the battlefield, Brutus defeats Octavius but Antony wins the day.
11
Both Cassius and Brutus commit suicide rather than allowing themselves to be taken prisoner.
12
Brutus is to be buried with honour and Rome is to be governed by those loyal to Caesar.

Summaries

General summary

Act I

The play opens on 15 February 44BC, the feast of Lupercalia. The ordinary citizens are celebrating Caesar's triumphs. Two tribunes, Murellus and Flavius, are incensed by the fickleness of the people.

Caesar's triumphal procession enters and a soothsayer warns Caesar to 'Beware the Ides of March' (I.2.15). Cassius is resentful of Caesar's popularity. This surprises Brutus and he admits that he too is unhappy that the people might choose to make Caesar king.

CHECK THE BOOK

Among the fiction that sheds some light on the time you will find *Antony* (1997) by Alan Massie.

Casca gives an amusing account of the manner in which Caesar refused the crown three times. Cassius reveals to the audience that he is planning to deceive Brutus into joining a plot against Caesar.

A terrifying storm breaks. Casca feels that the storm is a warning from the gods that something bad is about to happen. The assassination plot is already well developed.

Act II

It is now the Ides of March. Brutus is deeply troubled by the conflict between his feelings for Caesar and his fears about what he is doing to Rome. The conspirators visit Brutus at his house. Cassius wants to kill Caesar and his principal supporters. Brutus says the plot should involve only Caesar. This is agreed.

Portia shows her devotion to her husband and reveals her courage. This convinces Brutus that he should tell her of the plot to kill Caesar, but events prevent him from doing so. Calpurnia tells Caesar of a terrifying dream she has had. Caesar says that he will stay at home. Decius is desperate to take Caesar to the Senate and so interprets the dream as a good omen. Caesar believes him and goes to the Capitol. The conspirators arrive to escort him.

ACT III

Caesar approaches the Capitol accompanied by the conspirators. Artemidorus tries to give his petition to Caesar. The conspirators surround Caesar, stabbing and killing him. The final wound is inflicted by Brutus.

CHECK THE NET

Go to **www.greatbuildings.com** and look at the buildings of Ancient Rome in which the play is set.

Antony arrives and tells the conspirators that if they are going to kill him they should do so now. Brutus tells him that they mean him no harm. Antony then shakes the bloody hand of each of the conspirators. Brutus promises to give Antony good reasons why Caesar had to be killed. Antony asks to be allowed to give the oration at Caesar's funeral. Cassius does not want this but is overruled by Brutus.

Octavius, Caesar's great-nephew and heir, is coming to Rome. Antony plans to test the loyalty of the citizens of Rome in his speech at the funeral.

Brutus addresses the crowd, giving them a reasoned argument as to why Caesar had to die. Mark Antony then speaks. He constantly refers to the conspirators as 'honourable men' (III.2.87). Antony reads Caesar's generous will to the crowd. The crowd takes to the streets in their blind fury they kill Cinna the poet.

ACT IV

Antony, Octavius and Lepidus are in control in Rome. Brutus and Cassius, have fled to Sardis. Portia is dead. The Roman army under Antony and Octavius is marching on Philippi. Brutus overrules Cassius once again and the two rebels agree to lead their armies to Philippi to fight Antony and Octavius there. The ghost of Caesar appears to Brutus and says that he will see him again at Philippi.

CHECK THE BOOK

Extracts from Caesar's own *Commentaries on the Gallic Wars* can be found in many collections of writing from Ancient Rome.

ACT V

The generals meet on the battlefield. Once battle commences, Brutus is successful against Octavius whereas Cassius is defeated by Antony. Cassius orders his servant Pindarus to kill him. Brutus is then defeated and runs upon his own sword, killing himself. Mark Antony says that Brutus was 'the noblest Roman of them all' (V.5.68).

DETAILED SUMMARIES

SCENE 1 – The great feast

DID YOU KNOW?
Pompey had been defeated by Caesar four years earlier.

1 A great feast is held in Caesar's honour.

2 Not everyone is delighted at the public praising of Caesar.

A public area of Rome. Two tribunes, Flavius and Murellus, enter to find that a crowd has gathered. Flavius orders the crowd to disperse, saying that today is not a holiday. They are teased by a cobbler who gets the better of them by making **puns**. The cobbler says that people have gathered to rejoice in Caesar's triumph.

CHECKPOINT 1
Why are some Romans unhappy at Caesar's actions?

Caesar maintained his popularity by holding lavish public festivals. Here he has arranged a great celebration on the day of Lupercalia.

DID YOU KNOW?
The Lupercalia was a great Roman festival celebrating the earth's fertility.

This infuriates Flavius and Murellus who say that the same crowd that has now gathered to welcome home the victorious Caesar, once waited 'To see great Pompey pass the streets of Rome' (I.1.45). Murellus points out that Caesar has not brought any riches to Rome recently and so should not be treated as if he were a great victor returning with the spoils of war. Murellus is also incensed that Caesar should be worshipped when he was responsible for the fall of Pompey.

DID YOU KNOW?
A tribune was a magistrate from a plebeian (ordinary) family, elected to defend the interests of the plebeians against the power of the patricians.

Flavius and Murellus leave, vowing to remove any decorations from images of Caesar. It is the feast of Lupercalia and so many statues are 'decked with ceremonies' (scarves and ribbons) (I.1.68). Flavius feels that Caesar has grown too important for his own good.

SCENE 2 – Setting the scene

1 Caesar is warned by the soothsayer.

2 Cassius tries to enlist the help of Brutus in a conspiracy against Caesar.

3 Caesar turns down the crown of Rome three times.

4 Letters are forged to persuade Brutus.

On a street in Rome, Caesar, Calpurnia, Antony, Brutus and others are making their way to the races held to celebrate the feast of Lupercalia. Antony is to take part in the races and Caesar asks him to touch Calpurnia as he runs, in order to make her fertile (able to have children).

EXAMINER'S SECRET

Shakespeare has reduced the time between events. Lupercalia was actually held on 15 February; here it is the day before the Ides of March (15 March).

A soothsayer calls to Caesar from the crowd and Caesar turns to hear what he has to say. The soothsayer utters the famous line, 'Beware the Ides of March' (I.2.19). Caesar dismisses him as a dreamer and moves on.

CHECKPOINT 2

What is the dramatic point of the soothsayer?

CHECKPOINT 3

What does Brutus feel about Caesar?

Cassius and Brutus are left on stage and Cassius says that he has noticed how unhappy Brutus has looked recently. The cheers of the crowd at the games can be heard and Brutus lets slip that he is worried the people may be about to choose Caesar as king. Cassius is intrigued to hear that Brutus does not want Caesar to be king and tells him that he is also unhappy at Caesar's growing power.

An emperor would be regarded as both a king and a god.

It is **ironic** that the first words Brutus speaks in the play are to warn Caesar of the Ides of March: Brutus is to become a leading figure in the plot to assassinate Caesar on this very date.

Cassius tells Brutus of two occasions on which Caesar appeared to be very weak. Caesar had challenged Cassius to swim the River Tiber, which flows through Rome, with him. Cassius swam it easily but Caesar nearly drowned and had to be rescued, crying out 'Help me, Cassius, or I sink' (I.2.112). Cassius carried Caesar from the water. Later, when in Spain, Caesar developed a fever and cried 'As a sick girl' (I.2.129) for water. Cassius has seen Caesar at his weakest and cannot accept that he is supposed to treat him as a god.

CHECKPOINT 4

What do we learn here of Cassius's feelings towards Caesar?

Cassius goes on to say that Rome has not had one ruler for many years and that no single man should rule Rome. Brutus will not commit himself to this extent, but does say that he would rather be a villager than live in Rome under Caesar.

Caesar and his party enter. Caesar looks annoyed and immediately comments to Antony that he does not like the 'lean and hungry look' (I.2.194) he sees on the face of Cassius. Caesar does not trust him and says that, if he feared anyone, it would be Cassius.

Brutus stops Casca, one of the group that has been at the games, in order to find out what had taken place to cause the crowd to cheer so. Casca says that the crowd cheered as Antony offered the crown to Caesar. It was offered three times and each time Caesar refused it. It appeared to Casca that this had been deliberately staged and that Caesar was actually very reluctant not to take the crown. Caesar then fainted in the market-place after saying he would cut his own throat if the people of Rome asked him.

Cicero commented on the events, but spoke in Greek so that few could understand him. Murellus and Flavius have been 'put to silence' (I.2.287) for pulling scarves from statues of Caesar. Cassius, Casca and Brutus arrange to meet the following day. Cassius is not sure of Brutus's support. He decides to throw some messages, supposedly written by Roman citizens, through the window of Brutus's house, in the hope of swaying his opinion. The messages will praise Brutus and hint at Caesar's ambition.

CHECKPOINT 5

What does the treatment of Murellus and Flavius show of Caesar's methods?

Early ideas on Caesar and Rome

Note the way that Calpurnia and Antony address Caesar at the start of this scene. They treat him as their lord.

Romans worshipped their ancestors. The greater the ancestor, the more noble a Roman could claim to be.

Caesar refers to himself in the third person, i.e. 'Caesar' rather than 'I'.

Many important Romans wanted Rome to remain a republic. They strongly opposed the idea of there being a king again.

DID YOU KNOW?

A soothsayer was a fortune-teller.

DID YOU KNOW?

Cicero (106–43BC) was a famous speaker.

CHECKPOINT 6

How does Shakespeare tell the audience that an evil deed is coming?

SCENE 3 – The plot begins

1. **Rome is hit by terrible and unusual storms.**
2. **The conspirators meet and Cassius decides to ask for the help of Brutus.**

A street in Rome on a stormy night. Casca meets Cicero and describes various strange phenomena. He thinks they are omens that something terrible is about to occur. The things he has seen are:

- Fire dropping from the sky
- A slave who held up his hand which burst into flames, yet he was not burnt
- A lion which passed him in the street but did not seem to see him; men on fire walking the streets; a bird of night (probably an owl) at mid-day

Cassius enters as Cicero leaves. He has been walking about in the terrible storm, tempting fate by not sheltering from the lightning. He says that the strange events which have taken place are the result of heaven's impatience and that the world 'Incenses them to send destruction' (I.3.13). He likens the storms which have turned Nature upside down to Caesar's actions. Cassius tells Casca that Caesar, with his lust for power, is to blame for the upset in Nature. The many unnatural events described by Casca help to increase tension and would have emphasised to an Elizabethan audience that momentous events would occur.

Casca reveals that Caesar is to be crowned king by the senators on the following day. Cassius says that he would rather commit suicide using his own dagger, than live in Rome under Caesar. Romans considered it honourable to commit suicide.

CHECKPOINT 7

How might these messages trick Brutus?

Cassius has arranged to meet several important Romans at Pompey's monument. They are to discuss a matter of great importance and 'Of honourable dangerous consequence' (I.3.125). It is fitting that the conspirators should meet at Pompey's monument as Caesar defeated Pompey in battle to achieve power in Rome.

Cinna arrives, on his way to meet Cassius. He asks Cassius to attempt to enlist Brutus's support. Cassius has already thought of a way of persuading Brutus to help in the conspiracy to murder Caesar. He asks Cinna to place forged messages where Brutus will find them and to throw one in at his window. Casca comments that the presence of Brutus would change the people's opinion of the conspirators as Brutus is loved throughout Rome. Cassius is sure that he can persuade Brutus to join them and is quite prepared to lie to Brutus in order to enlist his help.

CHECKPOINT 8

Why do the conspirators feel the need to trick Brutus into joining them?

Many Romans feel they are behaving properly in ridding Rome of Caesar and thus preserving the Republic.

Now take a break! 

Test yourself (Act I)

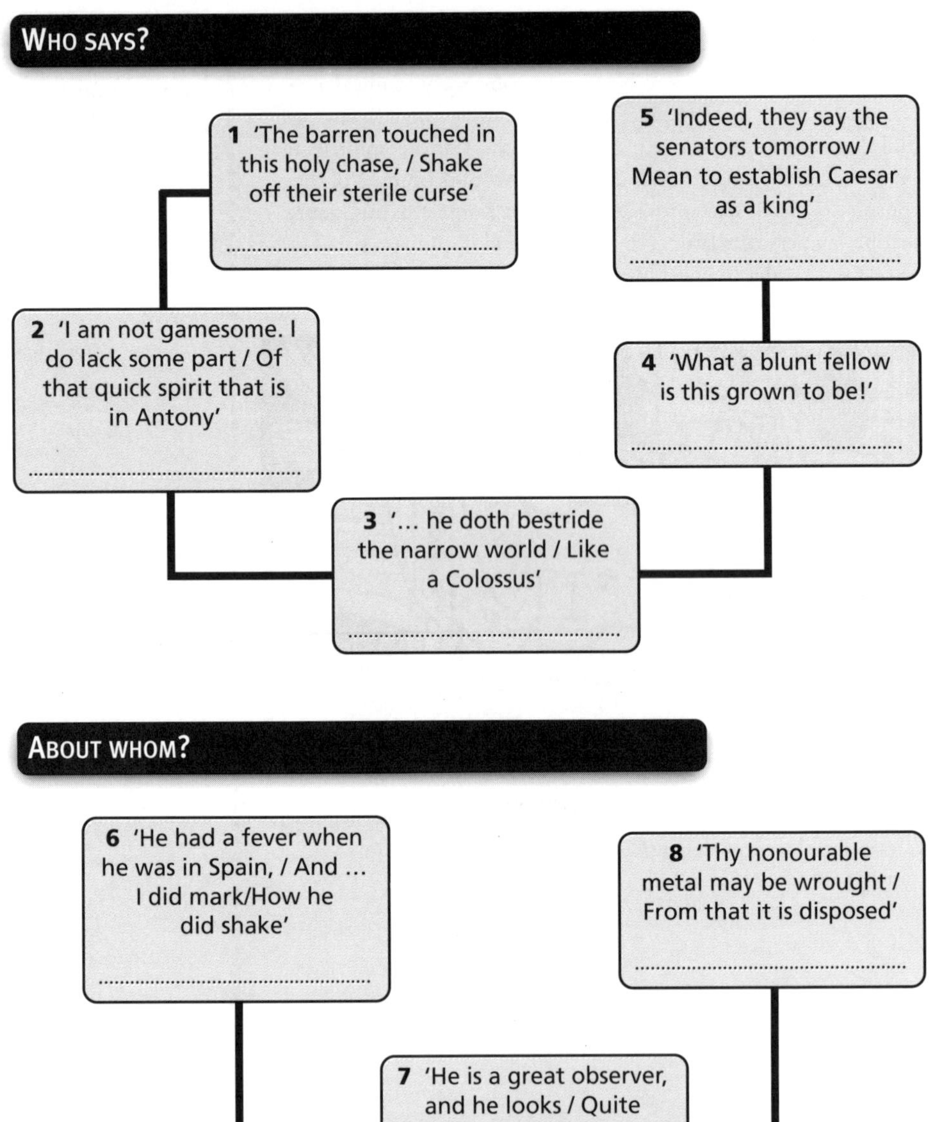

Who says?
1 'The barren touched in this holy chase, / Shake off their sterile curse'
2 'I am not gamesome. I do lack some part / Of that quick spirit that is in Antony'
3 '... he doth bestride the narrow world / Like a Colossus'
4 'What a blunt fellow is this grown to be!'
5 'Indeed, they say the senators tomorrow / Mean to establish Caesar as a king'
About whom?
6 'He had a fever when he was in Spain, / And ... I did mark/How he did shake'
7 'He is a great observer, and he looks / Quite through the deeds of men'
8 'Thy honourable metal may be wrought / From that it is disposed'

Check your answers on page 72.

SCENE 1 – The plot is finalised

1. **Brutus considers the murder of Caesar.**
2. **Brutus reads one of the false letters and is visited by Cassius.**
3. **The decision is taken not to harm Antony or any of Caesar's other followers.**

Brutus's villa at night. Brutus delivers a long **soliloquy** in which he debates the rights and wrongs of killing Caesar. Brutus says that he has no personal reason for wishing Caesar dead but that he fears what Caesar would become if he were crowned. Brutus compares Caesar's progress to an ambitious man climbing a ladder, saying that once he has reached the top he might turn his back on the ladder and look down upon everyone, 'scorning the base degrees / By which he did ascend' (II.1.26-7). He decides that Caesar must be killed now, before he attains complete power, just as it is easier to kill a serpent when it is in the egg than when it has hatched. Brutus does not respond quickly to the idea of killing Caesar.

CHECKPOINT 9

What does Brutus hint at here?

Lucius brings Brutus a paper which he has found by the window. Brutus asks if the Ides of March is tomorrow and then reads the letter. It tells him to 'awake' and to 'Speak, strike' redress' (II.1.46–55). He recalls that his ancestors drove the evil King Tarquin from Rome and decides that he must act in the same way. Lucius returns and tells his master 'fourteen days are wasted (passed)' (II.1.59) so that it is 15 March. Brutus has been troubled since Cassius first spoke to him against Caesar.

Lucius announces the arrival of Cassius and a group of men in disguise. Brutus remarks that not even Erebus (Hell) would be dark enough to hide the men who killed Caesar. Cassius wants the conspirators to swear an oath, but Brutus refuses, saying that that is the action of lesser men who need to give themselves reasons for action. Metellus says that he thinks the great orator, Cicero, should be involved but Brutus points out that Cicero would not be involved in something that he had not himself started.

CHECKPOINT 10

What is the main worry of Cassius?

Cassius suggests 'Let Antony and Caesar fall together' (II.1.161). Brutus is against this as he feels it would make the conspirators appear to be 'too bloody' (II.1.162) and more like butchers than sacrificers. Brutus makes a mistake in underestimating Mark Antony, believing he would be powerless without Caesar.

EXAMINER'S SECRET

Note the frequent use of the image of a snake or serpent throughout Brutus's **soliloquy**. The serpent has particular significance because of the story of Adam and Eve.

Cassius comments on Caesar's growing superstition and worries that he may take the events of the night as a warning and so not venture forth. Decius says that he will play on Caesar's superstitious nature and bring him to the Capitol. The conspirators leave Brutus alone and his wife, Portia, enters. She asks him why he has been so troubled lately and he replies that he has not been well. Portia says that he should, therefore, be in bed. She knows that he has met several people in secret and thinks his sickness is of the mind rather than the body. In order to prove her courage and her ability to keep a secret, she recently wounded herself in the thigh yet never complained of the pain. Brutus says 'Render me worthy of this noble wife!' (II.1.303) and promises to tell her everything. They are interrupted by a knock at the door. It is Caius Ligarius, come to join the conspiracy. Brutus leaves with him.

Kings in Rome

Many Romans were deeply suspicious of the idea of a king or emperor. Caesar was trying to grant himself powers that would have meant no one could ever challenge him. Even his closest friend, Brutus, realised that this could be very dangerous as no man could possibly handle such power.

The conspirators planned to act out of a love for Rome, though some were obviously acting out of simple jealousy.

Caesar's soldiers were probably quite happy for their general to be made emperor as this would have cemented their grip on Rome.

SCENE 2 – Caesar decides to visit the senate

1 Caesar and his wife have bad dreams.

2 Decius tricks Caesar into visiting the senate.

Caesar's house in the early morning of 15 March. Caesar has been disturbed by the storm and his wife has talked of murder in her sleep. He orders the priests to make sacrifices and to bring him news of the results.

DID YOU KNOW?

Many of Shakespeare's plays feature dreams. They were used to suggest a greater power was at work trying to warn the characters.

DID YOU KNOW?

Priests sacrificed animals, cut them open and believed they could make predictions by examining the state of the dead animal's organs.

CHECKPOINT 11

How does Decius trick Caesar here?

EXAMINER'S SECRET

Trebonius is behaving like a typical villain. He tells the audience of the evil deed he is preparing for.

Calpurnia asks Caesar not to leave the house but he says that he refuses to show fear. She tells him what she has heard of the night's strange events and feels that they can only indicate the death of someone great. News arrives from the priests; they have cut open a beast which had no heart – a very bad omen.

Caesar agrees to allow Mark Antony to go to the Senate and say that he is not well. Decius Brutus arrives and is told by Caesar that he will not be going to the Senate house. Caesar takes pains to point out that he chooses not to go to the Senate as opposed to being unable to go. Decius asks for a reason and tells Caesar that the senators will laugh at him otherwise. Caesar tells Decius of Calpurnia's dream, in which his statue ran with blood and Romans came to bathe their hands in it. Decius interprets the dream favourably, saying that it 'Signifies that from you great Rome shall suck / Reviving blood' (II.2.88–9).

Decius goes on to say that the Senate intend to crown Caesar today but that the senators might change their minds if Caesar does not appear and mock him for living by his wife's dreams. Caesar is taken in by the words of Decius and resolves to go. Brutus and several of the conspirators enter, followed by Mark Antony. Caesar asks Trebonius to stay close to him and Trebonius remarks, in an **aside**, 'And so near will I be / That your best friends shall wish I had been further' (II.2.126–7).

Brutus is troubled by his conscience, he is still unsure that he is taking the right course. He is merely acting like a friend and not actually being a friend to Caesar.

SCENE 3 – Possible warnings

❶ Artemidorus prepares to warn Caesar.

A street near the Capitol. Artemidorus is reading aloud a message that he has written. It is a warning to Caesar and gives the names of the conspirators, saying that they have no love for Caesar. Artemidorus decides to wait for Caesar to pass and then give him the message in the hope of saving his life.

SCENE 4 – Portia and the soothsayer

❶ Portia meets the soothsayer.

Outside Brutus's house. Portia tries to send Lucius on an errand to the Capitol to observe Brutus. She says she is worried about her husband's health and asks to be kept informed of anyone who approaches Caesar. A soothsayer enters and Portia questions him about his business. He tells her that he is waiting for Caesar as he fears for his safety. Portia finally sends Lucius to speak to Brutus, to say she is merry and to come back and tell her of his response.

This short scene, together with the previous one, establishes that Caesar may well be warned about the intended assassination, thus increasing the dramatic tension.

The soothsayer is delayed by Portia. This creates tension as he could warn Caesar. It is also **ironic** that he stops to speak to Portia of all people.

Now take a break!

Test yourself (Act II)

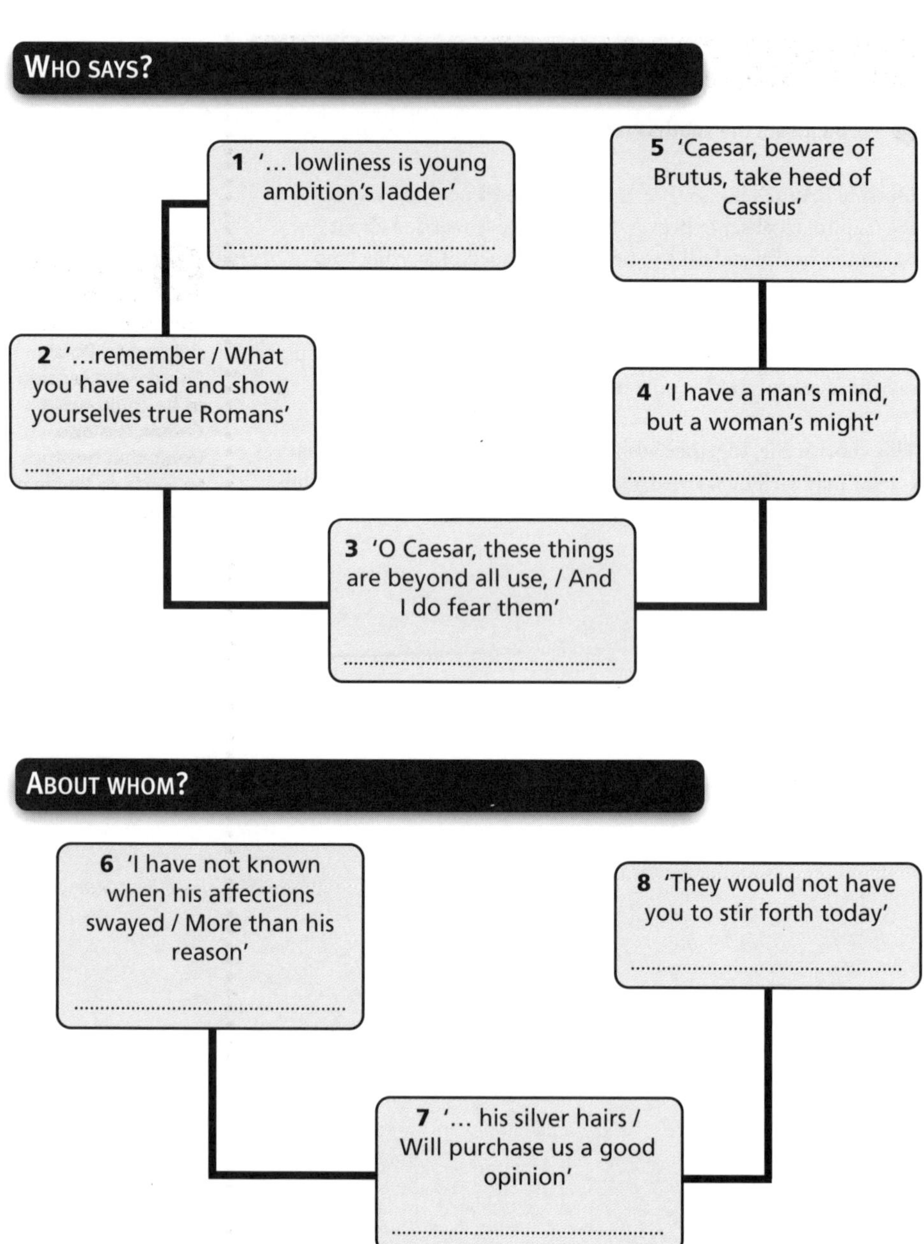

Who says?
1 '… lowliness is young ambition's ladder'
2 '…remember / What you have said and show yourselves true Romans'
3 'O Caesar, these things are beyond all use, / And I do fear them'
4 'I have a man's mind, but a woman's might'
5 'Caesar, beware of Brutus, take heed of Cassius'
About whom?
6 'I have not known when his affections swayed / More than his reason'
7 '… his silver hairs / Will purchase us a good opinion'
8 'They would not have you to stir forth today'

Check your answers on page 72.

SCENE 1 – The assassination of Caesar

1. **Caesar reaches the senate but is surrounded by the conspirators.**
2. **Caesar is stabbed by all of the conspirators, finally by Brutus.**
3. **Caesar dies.**
4. **Antony meets the murderers and is given permission to speak at the funeral of Caesar.**

A street close to the Capitol. Caesar enters with Brutus and the conspirators, Antony, Artemidorus, the soothsayer and other Romans. Caesar's first words in this scene have great impact because of the earlier conversation between Brutus and his servant. Caesar speaks of himself in the third person: 'Caesar'. This could be seen as a touch of arrogance on his part. Artemidorus gives Caesar his petition but Caesar does not read it because Decius gives him another. Artemidorus protests, saying that his is the more important as it affects Caesar directly, but Caesar says this is the very reason for reading it last.

Fate is clearly working against Caesar here.

The group enters the Capitol and Popillius, who seems to have found out about the plot, joins Caesar. This worries Cassius as he fears the conspirators are about to be caught, but Brutus assures him they are safe. Trebonius draws Antony away while Metellus approaches Caesar with a petition. Metellus wants his brother's banishment repealed but Caesar tells him not to beg. Brutus joins the appeal, kneeling at Caesar's feet, yet Caesar remains firm. He says 'But I am constant as the northern star' (III.1.61) – the one star which does not move in the heavens.

CHECKPOINT 12

Why does Metellus kneel in front of Caesar?

Caesar is attacked and stabbed many times. As Brutus attacks him he utters his last words 'Et tu Brute? – The fall Caesar!' (III.1.78) then dies. Caesar is killed at the foot of Pompey's statue. This is very **ironic** as Caesar himself defeated Pompey in battle to take power in Rome. Cinna and Cassius want to shout the news of their deed in the streets but Brutus prevents them from glorifying their actions.

The words 'Et tu, Brute?' are very famous. They reveal Caesar's surprise that even Brutus has attacked him.

GLOSSARY

Et tu, Brute? 'Even you, Brutus?'

Scene 1 continued

DID YOU KNOW?

An assassination such as this often led to mass retaliations against the dead man's followers.

Trebonius announces that Antony has fled. Brutus tells the conspirators to bathe their arms in Caesar's blood and show Rome that it is now free from tyranny. A servant arrives from Antony, bringing an offer of peace. Antony has asked that Brutus tell him why Caesar had to die and promises to follow Brutus if the answer is convincing. Cassius is worried about Antony.

CHECKPOINT 13

How does Antony reveal his true feelings for Caesar?

Antony enters and confronts Caesar's murderers. He says that if they intend to kill him then there is no better time than the present and no better weapons than those which killed Caesar. Brutus assures Antony that he will not be harmed and that he will explain his actions once the people of Rome have been told there is nothing for them to fear.

Antony makes a point of shaking the bloody hand of each of the murderers. Antony makes sure he knows who the conspirators are and makes a mental note of each man's name. Cassius has good reason to be worried about Antony. In this speech Antony calls some of the conspirators by two names. Romans generally had three names: the *praenomen*, like our Christian or first name; the *nomen*, the name of the clan; the *cognomen* which was the name of the family. It was rare for someone to use all three of their names, and as the play shows, most people were called by a single name. Antony's use of two names when speaking to some of the conspirators helps underline the tension of the occasion. He praises

Caesar and asks for his forgiveness for now befriending his killers. Cassius asks if Antony intends to be a friend to the conspirators. Antony says that he will be a friend to them if they can give him reasons why it was necessary for Caesar to die. Antony then asks for permission to 'Produce his body to the market place' (III.1.231) and to 'Speak in the order of his funeral' (III.1.234). Cassius is troubled by this as he fears what Antony might say, but Brutus decides to speak first and so assure the crowd of the need for Caesar's death. Brutus tells Antony not to blame the conspirators in his speech but to speak well of Caesar.

Antony is left alone with the body of Caesar. He says that this body is 'the ruins of the noblest man / That ever lived in the tide of times' (III.1. 259–60) and prophesies doom for those who killed him. Antony foresees bloody civil war and acts of great horror. He says that Caesar's spirit will 'Cry "Havoc" and let slip the dogs of war' (III.1.276) and that many dead men will need burying (only a king could 'Cry "Havoc"' and give the order for destruction). Antony's true intentions are revealed in lines 257–88. He speaks powerfully and the audience knows from this speech that his funeral **oration** will rouse the people of Rome.

CHECKPOINT 14

What does Antony tell the audience here?

A servant of Octavius enters and tells Antony that his master is approaching the city. Antony says that Octavius should wait outside the city until he has made his funeral **oration** and tested the loyalty of the people of Rome.

SCENE 2 – The funeral of Caesar

1. **Brutus wins the crowd to his side with his speech at Caesar's funeral.**
2. **Antony speaks more cleverly than Brutus and sways the crowd against Brutus and the others.**
3. **Antony reads Caesar's will over his corpse.**
4. **The crowd becomes a rioting mob and pursues the conspirators.**

The market-place in Rome. Brutus and Cassius enter with the ordinary people of the city. The two men arrange to speak separately to the people. Brutus addresses the crowd and tells them that he killed Caesar because he loved Rome even more than he loved Caesar. He asks them if they would rather be slaves and Caesar alive or freemen and Caesar dead. Brutus adds that he killed Caesar because of Caesar's ambition. When he asks the crowd whether anyone wishes to cease being a Roman in Rome as it is now, no one comes forward. Antony brings in the body of Caesar as Brutus offers the people of Rome his own life should they wish it. The people acclaim Brutus with one citizen saying 'Let him be Caesar' (III.2.53) as he leaves Antony to speak.

CHECKPOINT 15

How do the people see Brutus at the start of the scene?

Antony begins his address to a hostile crowd who are very much in favour of Brutus. The plebeians say that they are glad to be rid of Caesar and that Antony had better not say anything against Brutus.

He begins his speech by asking for their attention and says that he has not come to praise Caesar. Antony comments that a man's goodness dies with him but that his evil deeds live on after him. He refers to the statement that Brutus made about Caesar's ambition. Antony says if Caesar was ambitious 'it was a grievious fault, / And grieviously hath Caesar answered it' (III.2.83–4). He then refers to Brutus and the conspirators as honourable men, before repeating again that Brutus said Caesar was ambitious. Antony then gives examples of some of Caesar's actions:

- He brought many captives back to Rome whose ransoms filled the city's coffers.
- When the poor cried, Caesar wept with them.
- Caesar refused the crown three times.

CHECKPOINT 16

What does Antony set out to do?

These statements are punctuated by the comment that Brutus says Caesar was ambitious. Antony reminds the crowd that each person there loved Caesar at one time and so should now mourn his death.

This speech is well received by the crowd. Antony tells the people to remain loyal to the conspirators, who are, after all, honourable men. He then produces Caesar's will but says he dare not read it as it would prove how much Caesar loved the people of Rome. The crowd shouts for the will to be read. Antony refuses, saying that the will would only inflame the people; they insist that he reads it. Antony descends to the body of Caesar and asks the crowd to join him. By now the crowd has turned against Brutus and the conspirators whom they call traitors.

Antony lifts Caesar's cloak, torn by the conspirators' daggers, and shows it to the crowd. He says that the 'unkindest cut of all' (III.2.184) was made by Brutus whom Caesar loved. Antony describes the murder of Caesar and, finally, shows the people the body of Caesar. The people become enraged and swear vengeance upon the conspirators. Antony says that if he were a great orator such as Brutus, he would stir the people to avenge Caesar's death.

CHECKPOINT 17

Why are Antony's claims that he is a humble speaker clearly wrong?

Finally, he reads Caesar's will. Besides seventy-five drachmas for each citizen, Caesar has bequeathed his private gardens and orchards to the people. The crowd is now incensed and leaves with Caesar's body, saying that Caesar's funeral fire will be used to light torches to burn the houses of the traitors.

Octavius has arrived in Rome and Antony leaves to meet him at Caesar's house. Brutus and Cassius have fled the city.

The speeches

Brutus's speech is accepted by the crowd and, when he has finished speaking, the people are very much on his side. The speech of Brutus is in **prose** whereas Antony addresses the crowd in powerful **blank verse**.

The speech of Antony mirrors that given by Brutus. Antony cleverly sways the opinion of the crowd without attacking the conspirators directly. In his **oration**, Antony keeps repeating that Brutus is an honourable man, but follows this with statements intended to suggest the opposite.

After Antony's first speech the people begin to side with him. His speech by Caesar's body and the reading of his will are carefully calculated to turn the people against the conspirators. The speech brings about that which Cassius most feared – the people of Rome come to Antony's aid.

SCENE 3 – The mob takes to the streets

A street. Cinna, the poet, is confronted by a mob of angry citizens. They ask him many questions and when he tells them his name they kill him, because Cinna is the name of one of the conspirators.

CHECKPOINT 18

Why is the mob so angry?

This scene illustrates the fury of the mob. It also serves as a warning about the nature of vengeance and mob rule.

Now take a break!

Who says?

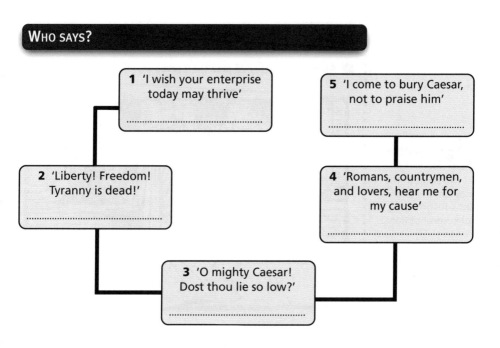

1 'I wish your enterprise today may thrive'

....

2 'Liberty! Freedom! Tyranny is dead!'

....

3 'O mighty Caesar! Dost thou lie so low?'

....

4 'Romans, countrymen, and lovers, hear me for my cause'

....

5 'I come to bury Caesar, not to praise him'

....

About whom?

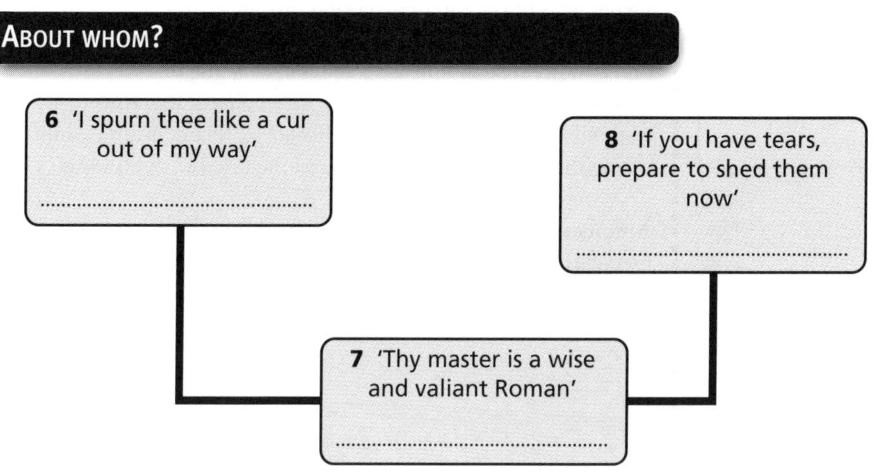

6 'I spurn thee like a cur out of my way'
7 'Thy master is a wise and valiant Roman'
8 'If you have tears, prepare to shed them now'

Check your answers on page 72.

SCENE 1 – Revenge is planned

❶ Antony and Octavius plan their revenge.

EXAMINER'S SECRET

At this point in the play Antony and Octavius are vying for control of Rome.

A nobleman's house. Antony, Octavius and Lepidus discuss which of the traitors must die. The list they draw up includes members of their own families. Once Lepidus leaves, Antony criticises him, saying he is fit only to be an errand boy and calling him 'a slight, unmeritable man' (IV.1.12). Octavius defends Lepidus, pointing out that Antony treated him as an equal in deciding that Lepidus's brother should be on the list of those who must die. Antony responds by likening Lepidus to his horse, finally insulting him by saying that Lepidus is always behind the times with his ideas.

CHECKPOINT 19

What do we learn of Antony's nature?

Antony says that Brutus and Cassius are raising an army and Octavius replies that they must prepare their own forces too. Octavius is worried that he and Antony have many secret enemies as well as those who are openly against them.

SCENE 2 – The camp of Brutus at Sardis

1 There is tension between Brutus and Cassius.

Brutus is unhappy with the actions of Cassius and some of his officers. Lucilius says that although Cassius received him with 'courtesy and respect enough' (IV.2.15), it was not with the warmth of earlier times. Cassius enters and accuses Brutus of having wronged him. Brutus tells Cassius not to speak like that in front of the soldiers. Brutus posts a guard outside his tent and he and Cassius remain inside.

SCENE 3 – Cassius and Brutus argue

1 Brutus and Cassius almost come to blows.

2 News arrives that Antony and Ocatvius have raised armies and are expected soon.

3 The ghost of Caesar visits Brutus.

Inside Brutus's tent. Cassius is angry with Brutus for having accused him of corruption. Brutus repeats the charge that Cassius has devalued their cause by selling official positions to undeserving people and suggests that Cassius is greedy. Cassius warns Brutus that if anyone else had said this, he would have killed him. Brutus reminds Cassius that they killed Caesar for the sake of justice and that they must not lose sight of the higher cause for which they acted. Cassius threatens Brutus who refuses to be intimidated. Brutus says that he will simply laugh at such foolish behaviour: 'I'll use you for my mirth, yea for my laughter' (IV.3.49).

Cassius becomes angrier and says that even Caesar would not have dared to stand up to him. Brutus counters this by saying that Cassius would never have argued with Caesar. Brutus tells Cassius that he is annoyed with him because when he asked Cassius for gold to pay his army, Cassius refused him. Cassius tries to pass this off as a misunderstanding and blames the messenger. He then says that one friend should accept the other's faults. Cassius offers his dagger

EXAMINER'S SECRET

The fact that Cassius and Brutus are beginning to doubt one another hints at their imminent failure.

CHECKPOINT 20

How does Brutus bring out the cowardice of Cassius?

to Brutus and tells him to cut out his heart rather than to scorn him. Brutus tells Cassius to put away his dagger and the two men shake hands as friends. There is discord in the rebels' camp. This fits in with the notion that they have done something wrong, an important element in Elizabethan drama.

A poet arrives to help the two generals resolve their quarrel. Brutus and Cassius laugh at him and send him away. Brutus now reveals that Portia is dead. Portia has committed suicide at the news that Antony and Octavius have joined forces. Her death puts Brutus under even more pressure than before.

Cassius marvels at the fact that Brutus did not kill him when they quarrelled earlier. Messala enters with news from Rome. He tells of many people killed on the orders of Antony, Octavius and Lepidus. He adds that Portia is dead, which Brutus already knows. Brutus takes the news of his wife's death, second time around, very calmly and so appears cold-hearted. However, many scholars believe that this is a mistake made when the original stage text was first printed. They think that Shakespeare intended only one of the discussions of her death to be included.

DID YOU KNOW?

Philippi was in Macedon, in what is now north-eastern Greece. It was, in fact, many hundreds of miles from Sardis, despite the impression given in the play.

Brutus and Cassius discuss the approach of the armies of Antony and Octavius and decide to intercept them at Philippi. Cassius is unhappy about this, but Brutus points out that the local people are

KPOINT 21

the replace-
f the eagle
other birds
nt?

POINT 22

e eagle
t to the

Cassius tells Messala of an omen he has seen: two eagles followed his army to Philippi and fed from the soldiers' hands, but that morning the eagles flew off and were replaced by ravens, crows and kites. Cassius and Brutus resolve not to allow themselves to be taken prisoner, though Brutus says that he will not commit suicide. Brutus and Cassius sound resigned to defeat, even though they eac put on a brave face.

Remember, the ghost of Caesar has promised to be at Philippi.

SCENE 2 – Battle commences

1. **Brutus attacks Octavius.**

The battlefield at Philippi. Brutus orders a messenger to tell the legions to attack the army of Octavius. He thinks that the troops of Octavius look in low spirits and not ready to fight. At this stage of the battle Brutus is hopeful of victory.

SCENE 3 – A case of mistaken identity

1. **Brutus is victorious but Cassius thinks the opposite.**
2. **Cassius asks his servant to kill him; Cassius dies.**
3. **Brutus finds Cassius dead.**
4. **Brutus realises he must fight Antony.**

NER'S

here.
he

Philippi, overlooking the battlefield. Cassius sees his soldiers fleeing from the battlefield. He notes that Brutus gave the order to attack too early. Pindarus, one of Cassius's servants, arrives and tells Cassius that Antony has entered his camp. Cassius asks his friend Titinius to ride to the camp to see whether the troops there are friend or enemy. Pindarus watches the progress of Titinius and reports that he has been taken prisoner. Cassius orders Pindarus to kill him with the same sword that he himself used to assassinate Caesar saying 'with this good sword, / That ran through Caesar's bowels, search this bosom' (V.3.41–2). Pindarus does so.

unsympathetic and that if they do not fight soon their army, which is at its peak, can only decline. Brutus takes a very philosophical view of life, comparing it to being afloat on a sea, pulled wherever the tide wishes.

Cassius leaves and Brutus has Lucius play him some music. Varrus and Claudio (two servants of Brutus) lie down in his tent to guard him. Eventually, Brutus is the only one awake and the ghost of Caesar enters. The ghost tells him that they will meet again at Philippi. Brutus wakes the others and sends word to Cassius that their armies should prepare immediately for battle. Ghosts were very important to Elizabethans who believed that a ghost would appear after an unnatural death and torment the person responsible for it.

EXAMINER'S SECRET

Ghosts were often used in Elizabethan drama to warn of the future.

Now take a break!

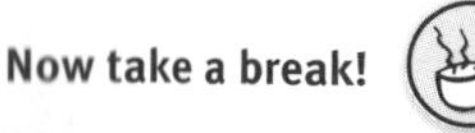

Test yourself (Act iv)

Who says?

1 '… we are at the stake / And bayed about with many enemies'

………………………………

2 'Before the eyes of both our armies here … / Let us not wrangle'

………………………………

3 'O ye gods, ye gods, must I endure all this?'

………………………………

4 'For certain she is dead, and by strange manner'

………………………………

5 'To tell thee thou shalt see me at Philippi'

………………………………

About whom?

6 'This is a slight, unmeritable man'

………………………………

7 '… you yourself / Are much condemned to have an itching palm'

………………………………

Check your answers on page 72.

Scene 1 – Preparing for battle

1. **Brutus and Cassius make a military mistake.**
2. **Cassius regrets letting Antony live.**
3. **Octavius and Antony compete for control.**

The battlefield at Philippi. Octavius and Antony have learnt that armies of Brutus and Cassius have marched to Philippi to meet t Octavius says that this has weakened the enemy's position as th have given up the high ground. Antony tells him that, by doing the enemy hope to appear brave, but that he is not fooled. Ant then tells Octavius to take the left-hand side of the battlefield l Octavius insists upon fighting on the right. In this argument Octavius is attempting to establish his superiority over Antor

The opposing generals meet to exchange words before the b begins. Antony rebukes Brutus for killing Caesar. He critic way they killed him while pretending to be his friends. Cas Brutus that, had he been allowed to kill Antony, these insu never have been uttered. Octavius swears to avenge the de Caesar and leaves with Antony.

Chec

Why is ment o by the significa

Check

Why is t importar Romans?

Exam Secre

Fate has acted against Cassius This is because killed Caesar.

The scene then switches to another part of the battlefield. Titinius has not been captured, he has met Brutus's victorious army which has defeated Octavius. Messala and Titinius go to tell Cassius the good news but find him dead. Titinius places a victory wreath on the head of Cassius and then kills himself with Cassius's sword.

Brutus enters to find both Cassius and Titinius dead. He remarks 'O Julius Caesar, thou art mighty yet' (V.3.94) and has made Brutus's friends turn their swords upon themselves. Brutus orders the body of Cassius to be taken to Thasos, an island off the nearby coast, because holding the funeral in camp would lower his soldiers' morale. He then tells his men to prepare for a second battle, this time against Antony's army.

CHECKPOINT 23

How is justice done in this scene?

The hand of fate

The Elizabethans believed in the idea that fate controlled the actions of humans. As soon as the conspirators kill Caesar, their fate is assured. Because Cassius and Brutus have killed Caesar they must be killed in order to avenge his death. (Of course the events in this play are also based upon historical fact.)

Fate can be seen to intervene when:

- Titinius has not been captured but has met soldiers from Brutus's victorious army. Pindarus misinterprets what he sees far off and, as a result, Cassius kills himself.
- Brutus comments about the power of Caesar's spirit. Certainly fate seems to have avenged his murder.

The Romans believed in fate too.

SCENE 4 – The battle continues

1 Antony seeks Brutus.

Another part of the battlefield. Cato and Lucilius are fighting soldiers from Antony's army. Cato is killed and Lucilius pretends to be Brutus. He admits the deception once Antony arrives. Antony tells his men to look after Lucilius and sets off to find Brutus.

Antony is impressed by the loyalty of Lucilius to Brutus.

SCENE 5 – Antony's victory and the death of Brutus

1. **Brutus has lost the day.**
2. **Brutus kills himself.**
3. **Antony and Octavius find the bodies of Cassius and Brutus.**

DID YOU KNOW?

'The pit' is a reference to a grave and to Hell.

CHECKPOINT 24

What does the manner of Brutus's death show of his character?

Near the battlefield at Philippi. Brutus and his remaining friends stop to rest. He asks first Clitus then Dardanius to kill him. They refuse. Brutus says that he has seen the ghost of Caesar again and knows that it is time for him to die. Volumnius refuses to accept this but Brutus says that he is defeated and has been driven 'to the pit' (V.5.23). He again asks the three men to help him die, but again they refuse. Brutus is left with his servant Strato, who was asleep during the earlier conversation. Brutus asks Strato to hold his sword and turn his face away while Brutus runs onto it. Strato shakes Brutus's hand and agrees. Brutus runs onto his own sword. His final words are that he killed himself more willingly than he had killed Caesar.

Elsewhere on the battlefield. Octavius and Antony enter with Messala and Lucilius. Strato tells them how Brutus died and Octavius asks the followers of Brutus to follow him now. Antony comments that Brutus was 'the noblest Roman of them all' (V.5.68) and says that only Brutus killed Caesar out of a sense of common good; all the others killed him out of envy. Antony praises Brutus for his virtue. Octavius says that Brutus will be given the funeral of a noble soldier.

Although the Romans regarded suicide as noble, the Elizabethans would have thought it dishonourable as they believed that only God had the power to take life.

Antony and Octavius behave in a noble way, forgiving those who fought against them.

The final outcome

Shakespeare is careful to show the audience that the murder of Caesar has not gone unpunished. This is not simply a case of sticking to historical facts. It would have been very dangerous for a playwright to have suggested that a 'king' could be murdered without any fear of reprisal. It was still thought that the King of England was appointed by God and that God would punish anyone who harmed his chosen representative on earth.

Now take a break!

CHECK THE NET

Find out about life in Elizabethan England at **www.renaissance.dm.net.** Alternatively type 'elizabethan + england' into your favourite search engine.

DID YOU KNOW?

Brutus is said to have had the perfect balance of the elements (earth, fire, air and water). The Elizabethans believed that a person's character was determined by the proportion of each of the elements in it!

Test yourself (Act v)

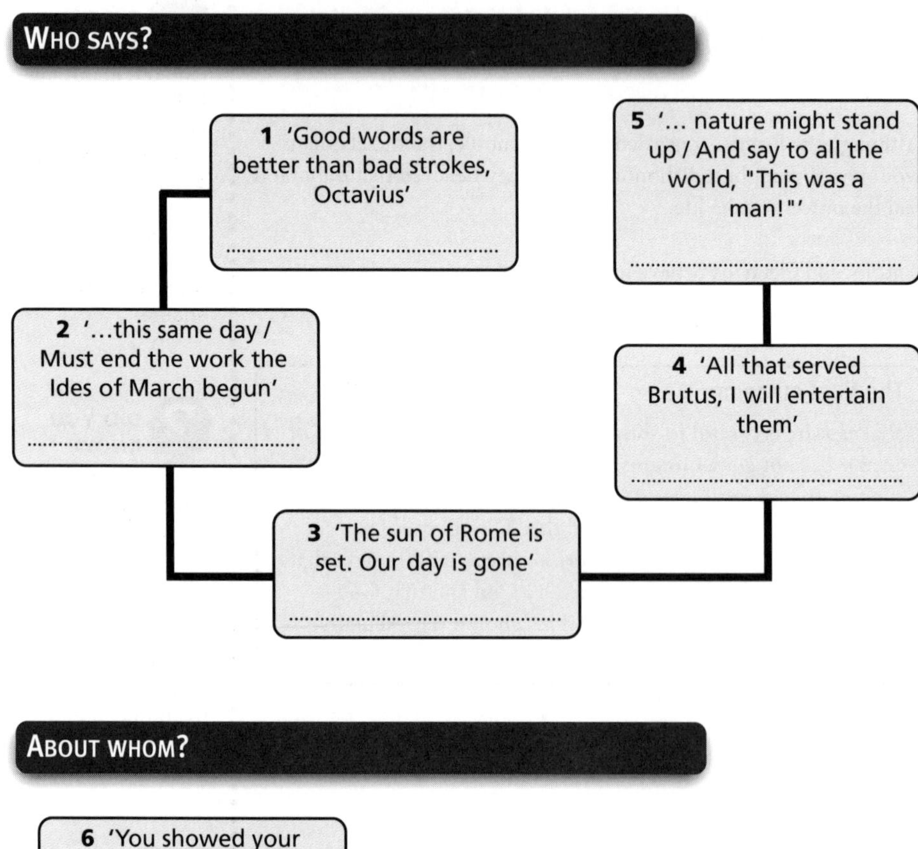

Who says?
1 'Good words are better than bad strokes, Octavius'
2 '…this same day / Must end the work the Ides of March begun'
3 'The sun of Rome is set. Our day is gone'
4 'All that served Brutus, I will entertain them'
5 '… nature might stand up / And say to all the world, "This was a man!"'

About whom?

6 'You showed your teeth like apes and fawned like hounds'

....

7 'Mark Antony is in your tents, my lord'

....

8 'This was the noblest Roman of them all'

....

Check your answers on page 72.

PART THREE

COMMENTARY

THEMES

POWER

The way that power affects the individual is an important theme. We see several major characters deal with the effects of power at various stages in the play.

EXAMINER'S SECRET

Shakespeare allows Caesar to reveal his own character through the rather pompous way he speaks.

Caesar

When the play opens Caesar is the most powerful man in Rome. It is clear that he has been in positions of power for some time because he speaks quite comfortably about his own high status. There are, however, clear signs in his own speech that Caesar has begun to be affected by his power.

He refers to himself in the third person, as 'Caesar', rather than in the first person, as 'I', suggesting that he has become rather full of his own importance. Some of the other characters speak of him as though he were a god. Antony says: 'When Caesar says "Do this!", it is performed' (I.2.10), a remark that shows that the commands of Caesar are law to many Romans.

Brutus

Brutus behaves differently. He says he is not interested in power for himself. He is concerned that power should be exercised properly. In the context of the play this means by the Republic which had a system of elected government. In reality, the Republic was not democratic. Many of the conspirators acted against Caesar because they were frightened of losing the control of the Senate that their families had held for generations.

Brutus is regarded as the senior member of the group that decides to kill Caesar and we see that Brutus does not use this power wisely. He overrules Cassius on three occasions, each with disastrous results. This shows that although Brutus has power he has neither the wisdom not the ruthlessness to use it properly. While there seems little doubt that both Caesar and Antony would have pursued their enemies, Brutus forgives his. His motivation is honourable but his opinion of Antony is a little naive.

DID YOU KNOW?

Rome was the most powerful state that the world had ever seen.

CHECK THE BOOK

Find out more about political intrigue in Rome in *I, Claudius* (1976) by Robert Graves.

Mark Antony

Mark Antony is a follower of Caesar in more ways than one. After Caesar's death, Antony tries to act as he thinks Caesar would have done and is prepared to use his abilities to stir up the masses. Antony's power over the people is similar to that of Caesar's, as is his manipulation of the populace to serve his own ends.

Antony realises that he can be given power by the people of Rome, whereas he is unable to seize power by force. Once he has the power given by the enraged masses he uses it ruthlessly to crush his enemies. He makes better military decisions than any of the other generals at Philippi, yet allows Octavius to assume power. (Twelve years later Antony was defeated by Octavius at the battle of Actium.)

Octavius

Octavius behaves as though it is natural for him to take control in Rome following the death of Caesar. Although he is supposedly in partnership with Antony (and Lepidus), Octavius insists on taking the more favourable side of the battlefield at Philippi. Antony lets him, suggesting that Antony recognises the superiority of Caesar's great-nephew. Shortly after the battle of Philippi, Octavius went to war against Antony and eventually defeated him. Octavius took the name Augustus and became the first Roman Emperor. He certainly understood the nature of power.

LOYALTY

To the state

The murder of Caesar takes place for both personal and public reasons, yet there are sufficient public reasons alone for Brutus to join the conspiracy. Roman noblemen were fiercely proud of their republican status and opposed a return to monarchy. The idea that the state encompassed everyone and acted in the common good was one that many senior Romans looked to as the example of good government.

DID YOU KNOW?

The US government is based directly upon that of ancient Rome with a senate and senators.

In reality, the government of Ancient Rome was little better than a modern dictatorship because ordinary people had no say in what was decided in their name. The important positions in Rome had been held by members of the same few families for years and so the notion of a people's republic was something of a sham.

All the actions in the play are carried out in the name of Rome. Each man adapts this notion of loyalty to the state to suit his own cause: Cassius to remove Caesar, of whom he is jealous; Antony to avenge his murdered friend.

Antony is loyal to the Rome that he knew under Caesar; a powerful nation made wealthy by conquest. Brutus is loyal to the notion of a republic, though was himself a member of a powerful and wealthy family.

It is no accident that all those characters who are disloyal to the state end up dead. This is because of the political climate when the play was written and first performed. A playwright dare not suggest that the murder of a king, or even a near king, would be allowed to go unpunished. Of course the events actually took place, but there is more than historical fact at work here. The conventions of Elizabethan England insisted that perpetrators of regicide (the murder of a king) should suffer.

The good reader might dip into *The History of the Decline and Fall of the Roman Empire* by Edward Gibbon (1761).

To friends

The close personal relationships that exist between some of the characters are also factors in determining their actions. Antony acts largely out of a desire for personal revenge upon Caesar's killers. His close friendship is very important to him and is a major element of his motivation in pursuing Caesar's killers. Caesar had trusted Antony, as can be seen when he asked Antony to touch Calpurnia in the race at the festival of Lupercalia. The two men had fought many campaigns together and knew one another very well.

Shakespeare took several of his history plays from the stories in *Plutarch's Lives*.

Brutus is friendly with Cassius and allows this friendship to cloud his judgement at times. Brutus is also aware of his own personal friendship with Caesar. Shakespeare is careful to observe the account of Caesar's death given by Plutarch in which Brutus strikes the fatal blow. This friendship affects Brutus greatly and he finds it difficult to overcome his feelings of personal grief at the death of Caesar.

Personal wishes are, however, seldom allowed to interfere with the larger issues at stake. The major characters in the play are all statesmen and understand, though to different degrees, the role of friendship and the use of power.

Within marriage

Two married couples appear in the play: Caesar and Calpurnia, and Brutus and Portia. The two relationships are in marked contrast. Caesar and Calpurnia seem to have a rather formal marriage. He is very much in charge, though he does show consideration for his wife's opinions when he decides to stay at home on the morning of the Ides of March. He is not relaxed enough with his wife to drop the habit of calling himself 'Caesar'. Perhaps this is intended to show his importance, but it does tend to make him appear a vain and inconsiderate husband.

This is all part of the convention of **tragedy**. Caesar has to have a major fault (vanity) in order to bring about his downfall.

Brutus and Portia, however, have a very close, trusting relationship. She goes to great lengths to prove her loyalty to her husband, wounding herself in the thigh and not complaining about it to prove she can bear great hardship when required to. He intends to tell her of the plan to kill Caesar and this is the only example in the play of a man really letting a woman into his world. This marriage is much more of an equal partnership (at least in Elizabethan terms) than that between Caesar and Calpurnia.

Now take a break!

STRUCTURE

The events of the play take place over three days. In real life this would not be possible, because it would have taken weeks for the armies to reach Philippi. On stage, however, the three-day model works very effectively. Each day is neatly split into sections from morning until night, as follows:

Day one

In the morning the people take to the streets to praise Caesar.

In the afternoon the games of the Lupercalia festival are held and Cassius approaches Brutus about joining the conspiracy.

At night there are terrible storms as the conspirators discuss the plot at Brutus's house.

Day two

In the morning Calpurnia tells Caesar of her dream. He then goes to the Senate with the conspirators and is killed shortly afterwards.

In the afternoon Antony stirs up the crowd against the conspirators at Caesar's funeral.

In the evening Octavius, Lepidus and Antony meet. Brutus and Cassius argue then reconcile their differences.

Day three

In the morning the generals meet.

In the afternoon the battle begins.

In the evening Cassius commits suicide and Brutus kills himself that night.

Although nonsense in terms of the real passage of time, by reducing the action to three days, Shakespeare gives the audience a clearly defined time frame, so making the action seem more realistic. It also adds to the urgency and dramatic tension of the play as matters have to be resolved in such a short time.

CHECKPOINT 25

How does this structure reflect the duration of the play on stage?

CHARACTERS

JULIUS CAESAR

The Caesar that we see at the opening of the play is the greatest and most powerful man in Rome. He has defeated Pompey, his closest rival, and has effectively taken charge of the empire. The only thing he lacks is the crown. Caesar is ambitious, yet he can also be very human. His first concern in the play is that Antony, when running in the race at the festival of the Lupercalia, should touch Calpurnia so that she might conceive a child. He appears here to be a considerate man, affected by the same everyday concerns as anyone else. However this concern could also be interpreted as vanity: he is ageing (see below) and has no heir, so would appear still young and virile if his wife became pregnant.

Ruthless
Powerful
Ambitious
Manipulative
Vain

We hear from Cassius that Caesar has started to behave as if he were a god. This might simply be jealousy on the part of Cassius, a man whom Caesar did not favour. There must be some truth in it because Brutus becomes involved in the conspiracy.

Caesar is clearly ambitious and Casca's amusing account of the scene at the Lupercalia games, where Caesar refused the crown when he obviously wanted to accept it, shows us this. He speaks of himself as being different to ordinary men, telling Metellus that he, Caesar, does not act unjustly and cannot be swayed as other men might be. This suggests a certain arrogance on his part. It is clear in this scene (Act III, Scene 1) why some men feel aggrieved at Caesar's self-importance. His constant references to himself in the third person add to this impression.

DID YOU KNOW?

The name of Caesar was so important that the Roman emperors who followed him also called themselves 'Caesar'.

Caesar's vanity is clear when he decides to go to the Capitol in order to avoid being laughed at. This is another side of Caesar which shows weakness. He is far from the invincible, god-like creature he wishes to appear. Caesar has physical weaknesses too: his epilepsy, fevers and partial deafness show him to be more frail than he would have people think. Shakespeare has chosen to portray Caesar as an ageing man. This certainly makes him more human and more believable.

MARCUS BRUTUS

Marcus Brutus is widely regarded as a noble man. He is a friend of Caesar and is forced to examine his conscience closely over the assassination of a man he loves and respects. Brutus is something of an idealist. He believes in the Republic as the best form of government. Because of his love for Rome he allows himself to be drawn into the plot to kill Caesar. Antony remarks that Brutus was the only one of the group who did not kill Caesar because of envy and personal grievance. Brutus acted in what he thought were the best interests of Rome.

Honourable
Idealistic
Courageous
Loving
Trusting

Brutus proves himself to be a poor judge of character as he places too much trust in Cassius. He is flattered by the words that apparently came from anonymous citizens and so shows that, like Caesar, he can be vain. Though he believes what Cassius later tells him, Brutus does not allow the murder of Caesar to become a massacre of his supporters too. He restrains Cassius and the others, even over the fate of Mark Antony. This proves fatal.

EXAMINER'S SECRET

Be prepared to examine the character of Brutus in some depth. He acts out of a sense of honour and is a very complex character.

Of all the men in the play, Brutus is the only one whose domestic life we see much of. His very close relationship with Portia is in contrast to the more formal one between Caesar and Calpurnia. Brutus shows his courage when accepting the news of Portia's death. This courage also manifests itself in his suicide when all is lost at Philippi. He dies in a manner that Romans would have thought brave and avoids the humiliation of being led through the streets of Rome as a prisoner.

Brutus lets his idealism overcome his reason and pays the price for it.

CASSIUS

At the start of the play Cassius is a mean man, consumed by jealousy. He resents the fact that Caesar shows him no favour and is clearly envious of Caesar's growing power and popularity. There is little in him to make the audience feel sympathy for his cause.

EXAMINER'S SECRET

Cassius likes to tempt fate but he goes too far with the murder of Caesar. Be prepared to comment on Cassius and fate.

Cassius is easily excited, yet proves to be a better judge of character and of strategy than the more placid Brutus. Cassius

Jealous
Scheming
Impulsive
Good strategist
Quick-tempered

plots Caesar's murder and is responsible for recruiting the conspirators. The judgements of Cassius regarding the killing of Antony and the fighting of a battle at Philippi prove to be more sound than those of Brutus. Even so, he takes unnecessary risks, such as walking the streets during the storm, tempting the lightning to strike him.

As the play develops, and particularly after the death of Caesar, Cassius becomes a more sympathetic character. At Philippi he is able to console Brutus over the death of Portia. His friendship with Brutus redeems him as a man and causes the audience to warm to him. His death is tragic as it occurs because of his hot-headedness. He is a complex character, capable of the full range of human emotions.

MARK ANTONY

Ruthless
Loyal
Shrewd
Emotional
Calculating

Until the death of Caesar, Antony is little more than a follower. He is a friend to Caesar, in much the same way that Cassius is to Brutus. Antony has been a successful soldier and is underestimated by Brutus. His character becomes really defined when he gives the stirring oration over Caesar's body, and shows a new side of himself. He is a skilful orator and easily turns the crowd to his way of thinking. He shows that he has a logical mind and that he can be ruthless when in pursuit of the enemy.

This ruthless side comes to the fore when he is trading the lives of the traitors for his own political ends. The death of Caesar, his beloved friend, brings out characteristics in Antony which he has doubtless used before in battle, but which we did not see in the first half of the play. The chillingly calculating avenger emerges from the funeral of Caesar and he proves himself to be a powerful statesman. Interestingly, he allows Octavius to overrule him at Philippi, though this is possibly due to loyalty to Julius Caesar who had appointed Octavius his heir. Antony is also shrewd enough to avoid a split in the Roman forces just before a major battle. Although he takes the inferior side of the battlefield he is victorious, whereas Octavius is defeated.

Antony is driven by his emotions and will not allow anything or anyone to stand in the way of what he feels to be right. In this way he could be said to be similar to Brutus. Antony has a savage streak which Brutus lacks and it is this savagery which leads him to victory and ensures that he avenges Caesar's murder. Antony proves himself to be a great leader of men, a powerful public speaker and a cunning politician.

CHECK THE FILM

A famous account of Antony's life after the events of this play is *Cleopatra* (1963) starring Richard Burton and Elizabeth Taylor. (It was the most expensive film ever made.)

CALPURNIA

Calpurnia is a level-headed woman who does not normally let herself be influenced by superstition. She shows her affection for her husband on the morning of the Ides of March when she attempts to prevent him going to the Capitol. Calpurnia is intelligent and recognises that Caesar has become overconfident. She is worried by her dream, but also by the fact that Caesar seems to be beginning to believe that he is invincible. She does not seem to have any ambition for herself and does not show any sign of being impressed by Caesar's imminent promotion to king.

PORTIA

Portia is portrayed as a good Roman wife. She is loyal and caring towards Brutus and would clearly go to any lengths to protect him. She is a passionate woman as shown by her action to prove she can keep a secret. Wounding herself in the thigh is a drastic act, but is very much the behaviour of someone who can easily allow passion to overrule reason. She is a good contrast to the colder Brutus.

Ultimately it is this passion and loyalty which are her undoing. Unable to contemplate life without Brutus, she swallows hot coals and dies in a typically **tragic** manner.

CASCA

Casca is a cynical man; he is in fact a Cynic. Followers of this school of Greek philosophy believed that virtue is the only good and that it can only be achieved by individual self-control, and not by imposed social conventions. The account he gives of the Lupercalia games is humorous and dry. He has little time for pretence and is very cutting in his remarks about Caesar's behaviour. He is portrayed as straight-talking and shows little emotion when first we meet him. However, Casca is not so impervious to superstition as he would like us to believe. He is terrified by the storm and becomes excited when recounting the strange things he has seen.

DECIUS BRUTUS

It is Decius who raises the question of killing Caesar's followers as well as Caesar himself. He is also the man who flatters Caesar sufficiently to bring him to the Capitol. Decius is a skilful and persuasive speaker. He obviously knows Caesar's weaknesses and is intelligent enough to use them to get what he wants. Decius expects Caesar to accompany him to the Capitol rather than let himself be laughed at. This shows a certain shrewdness in his nature.

OCTAVIUS CAESAR

Octavius eventually turned on Antony and his forces defeated Antony in Eqypt.

Octavius is the heir to Julius Caesar's wealth and position. He is the great-nephew of Julius Caesar and regards himself as successor to power in Rome. He is not as good a general as Antony, but still insists on ordering the battle lines at Philippi. His character is not clearly defined but he shows something of the nature that will enable him to become Augustus Caesar. He is clear in his own mind and will not be dissuaded once he has made a decision. This is a potential weakness, yet he shows many of Julius Caesar's qualities when dealing with people.

Now take a break! 

LANGUAGE AND STYLE

Julius Caesar contains powerful and striking language. The Elizabethan view of Ancient Rome as a place of great nobility and honour is reflected in the speech of the characters in the play. Shakespeare makes great use of rich **imagery** to create the world of Rome on the stage. The play is full of references to the buildings and statues of Rome, creating an impression of a place which is cultured and powerful.

Students make common errors when starting to talk about the writer's use of language. It is probably one of the more difficult aspects of literature. In this section you will be given some information about the language used by Shakespeare and some pointers as to how to go about discussing it.

The first thing about the language used in *Julius Caesar* is that it is all speech. This may seem an obvious thing to say about a play but there are rules about the type of speech used at certain times and by certain characters.

There are two different types of speech used in the play:

- **Blank verse**
- **Prose**

Most of the characters speak in blank verse. This is different from the way we normally speak. Verse has a rhythm, meaning that all the lines follow the same pattern.

Verse is a convention that would have been recognised by the audience.

Here is a line of verse from the play: 'Thou art the ruins of the noblest man' (III.1.259).

The line has ten beats to it, in its arrangement of stressed and unstressed syllables. The line which follows it also has ten beats to it: 'That ever lived in the tide of times' (III.1.260).

These are examples of **blank verse**. It is called 'blank' because it does not rhyme. This type of speech is used in two situations:

- Formal speech between important characters
- When something important is being said

Blank verse might seem rather an unusual convention to us but consider some conventions that we take for granted:

- Television advertisements are around thirty seconds long
- Music chart singles are rarely over three minutes long
- No matter what happens to Superman he will always come out on top

We accept these conventions because we have grown used to them or indeed never known anything else. Shakespeare's audience would have been comfortable with the stage conventions of the day.

DID YOU KNOW?
Verse is much easier to learn than prose.

Occasionally, a character speaks in rhyme. This is to let the audience know either that something important is being said or that a scene is about to end. Remember, there were not the breaks in performance due to lighting changes that we have in the theatre today. Plays were performed in the open air and in daylight. Rhyme was one device that could assist the audience in recognising an important element of the play.

When we speak in everyday situations we do not speak in blank verse. Imagine how difficult it would be if everything we said had to be fitted into a pattern like the one above. What we would think of as normal speech is called **prose**. There are clear situations in which prose is used:

- When characters are relaxed and talking about unimportant matters
- By unimportant characters
- By uneducated characters in order to make them seem rather rough

The way in which a character uses language helps the audience to decide what sort of person he/she is. Here are some examples of different uses of language:

- Caesar speaks very formally, even with his wife, and seems unable to relax.
- The phrase, 'Beware the Ides of March' is repeated several times in Act I, Scene 2. This is to emphasise its importance. Caesar even reflects on it in Act III, Scene 1, shortly before his death, 'The Ides of March are come.' (III.1.1)
- Antony deliberately repeats the phrase 'Honourable men' throughout his speech to the people of Rome in Act 3 Scene 2. This is of course to suggest that Brutus and the conspirators are anything but honourable.
- Antony uses deliberate exaggeration or **hyperbole** in his speech in Act III, Scene 2 in order to inflame the citizens of Rome:

'O, what a fall was there, my countrymen!
Then I, and you, and all of us fell down'

(III.2.191–2)

Antony's speech is an example of rhetoric. Remember to comment on this.

Interestingly, the funeral speech made by Brutus is in prose, perhaps to signify his wish to communicate with ordinary people. In contrast, when Antony speaks to the crowd in his famous 'Friends, Romans, countrymen' speech he uses verse.

Consider the effectiveness of the two opening lines:

- Brutus: 'Romans, countrymen, and lovers, hear me for my cause, and be silent, that you may hear.' (III.2.13–14)
- Antony: 'Friends, Romans, countrymen, lend me your ears!
I come to bury Caesar, not to praise him.' (III.2.77–8)

Antony's speech is full of high poetry, for example, 'O judgement! Thou art fled to brutish beasts, / And men have lost their reason.' (III.2.108–9)

He makes self-contained statements about the greatness, kindness and honour of Caesar and then adds that the conspirators are 'honourable men'. This use of reasoned argument is known as **rhetoric**. Elizabethan schoolchildren studied rhetoric and it was considered a good way of demonstrating how clever (witty) you were.

Prose is used by Casca when he gives his account of Caesar's refusal to take the crown at the games. This use of informal language allows the character to develop the humour of the situation. It also tells the audience that Casca does not take Caesar seriously.

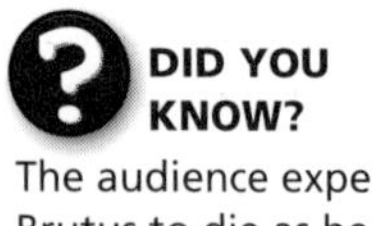

The audience expect Brutus to die as he has killed the rightful leader.

One other notable use of language is in the way Julius Caesar refers to himself in the third person. He calls himself 'Caesar' instead of 'I'. Even when speaking to his wife he says 'Caesar shall forth' (II.2.10). This has two effects: it distances Caesar from the rest of the characters and makes him sound rather pompous and self-important.

The way that Brutus is resigned to his fate at the end of the play is reliant upon verse. The powerful emotions he expresses are more suited to verse than to prose, e.g. 'Night hangs upon mine eyes, my bones would rest' (V.5.41).

When you are talking about language try to understand why the writer has used particular words and phrases. Is Hamlet's famous line, 'To be or not to be, that is the question' (III.1.56) more effective than 'Should I kill myself?' Most people would say so but you have to look at why.

Style is all in the way that the thing is said. Some writers are simply better at this than others.

Remember the following points about any text you read:

- The writer started off with a blank page.
- Every word has been written – it is not real. (You could say that the text is a **construct**.)
- One form of words may be far more effective than another in getting across a particular idea or feeling.

- The writer set out to do something – not simply to fill the page – you have to identify what this aim was.
- You should discuss whether the writer has been effective, e.g. is a frightening passage actually frightening?

Finally, try to develop an appreciation for style. This can only be done by reading the work of different writers. You need to have your own opinion as to how good Shakespeare is at expressing ideas and emotions.

Remember that you will be writing about the play as both a piece of writing and a drama intended for performance.

Now take a break!

PART FOUR

RESOURCES

Your use of quotations is one of the most revealing things about you. Skilful use of quotations suggests a high level of understanding of the play.

HOW TO USE QUOTATIONS

One of the secrets of success in writing essays is the way you use quotations. There are five basic principles:

1. Put inverted commas at the beginning and end of the quotation.
2. Write the quotation exactly as it appears in the original.
3. Do not use a quotation that repeats what you have just written.
4. Use the quotation so that it fits into your sentence.
5. Keep the quotation as short as possible.

When you use quotations in this way, you are demonstrating the ability to use text as evidence to support your ideas - not simply including words from the original to prove you have read it.

Your comment should not duplicate what is in your quotation. For example:

> **Antony says that his heart is in the coffin with Caesar: 'My heart is in the coffin there with Caesar' (III.2.110).**

Far more effective is to write:

> **Antony shows the crowd how much he has been hurt by Caesar's death: 'My heart is in the coffin there with Caesar' (III.2.110).**

Always lay out the lines as they appear in the text. For example:

> **'... Danger knows full well**
> **That Caesar is more dangerous than he' (II.2.45-6)**

However, the most sophisticated way of using the writer's words is to embed them into your sentence:

Cassius says that he has seen the mighty Caesar cry 'As a sick girl' (I.2.129) and reminds Brutus that 'this god did shake' (I.2.122) when he had a fever.

When you use quotations in this way, you are demonstrating the ability to use text as evidence to support your ideas - not simply including words from the original to prove you have read it.

COURSEWORK ESSAY

Set aside an hour or so at the start of your work to plan what you have to do.

- List all the points you feel are needed to cover the task. Collect page references of information and quotations that will support what you have to say. A helpful tool is the highlighter pen: this saves painstaking copying and enables you to target precisely what you want to use.
- Focus on what you consider to be the main points of the essay. Try to sum up your argument in a single sentence, which could be the closing sentence of your essay. Depending on the essay title, it could be a statement about a character: Brutus is a noble man. He feels that he is acting in the best interests of the people of Rome; an opinion about setting: It is quite fitting that the conspirators meet at the statue of Pompey to discuss the murder of Caesar; or a judgement on a theme: The effects of power upon the individual is an important theme in the play.
- Make a short essay plan. Use the first paragraph to introduce the argument you wish to make. In the following paragraphs develop this argument with details, examples and other possible points of view. Sum up your argument in the last paragraph. Check you have answered the question.
- Write the essay, remembering all the time the central point you are making.
- On completion, go back over what you have written to eliminate careless errors and improve expression. Read it aloud to yourself, or, if you are feeling more confident, to a relative or friend.

Examiners know the play so they do not need to be told the story. Refer to aspects of the plot – do not write it out in detail.

Keep checking on the wording of the question as you write. This will stop you drifting off the point.

If you can, try to type your essay, using a word processor. This will allow you to correct and improve your writing without spoiling its appearance.

SITTING THE EXAMINATION

Examination papers are carefully designed to give you the opportunity to do your best. Follow these handy hints for exam success:

BEFORE YOU START

Read the entire exam paper before deciding which question to answer.

- Make sure you know the subject of the examination so that you are properly prepared and equipped.
- You need to be comfortable and free from distractions. Inform the invigilator if anything is off-putting, e.g. a shaky desk.
- Read the instructions, or rubric, on the front of the examination paper. You should know by now what you have to do but check to reassure yourself.
- Observe the time allocation – and follow it carefully. If they recommend 60 minutes for Question 1 and 30 minutes for Question 2, it is because Question 1 carries twice as many marks.
- Consider the mark allocation. You should write a longer response for 4 marks than for 2 marks.

WRITING YOUR RESPONSES

- Use the questions to structure your response, e.g. question: 'The endings of X's poems are always particularly significant. Explain their importance with reference to two poems.' The first part of your answer will describe the ending of the first poem; the second part will look at the ending of the second poem; the third part will be an explanation of the significance of the two endings.
- Write a brief draft outline of your response.
- A typical 30-minute examination essay is probably between 400 and 600 words in length.
- Keep your writing legible and easy to read, using paragraphs to show the structure of your answers.

- Spend a couple of minutes afterwards quickly checking for obvious errors.

WHEN YOU HAVE FINISHED

- Don't be downhearted – if you found the examination difficult, it is probably because you really worked at the questions. Let's face it, they are not meant to be easy!
- Don't pay too much attention to what your friends have to say about the paper. Everyone's experience is different and no two people ever give the same answers.

IMPROVE YOUR GRADE

Whatever text you are studying, it is vital that you are really familiar with its contents. These Notes are intended to help you find your way around *Julius Caesar* but they are not a substitute for reading and watching the play.

Keep your handwriting neat and legible.

You need to develop a good knowledge of two major aspects of the play:

THE PLOT: Make sure that you know the order of events and how references early in the play affect events later on.

THE CHARACTERS: Make sure you know who's who and what the various characters do and say.

Most students can immediately make some improvement in grade by recognising what it is that they are being asked to do. All written tasks can be broken down into the following simple areas:

- AIMS: What did the writer set out to do?
- MEANS: How did the writer go about doing it?
- SUCCESS: Was the writer successful?

AIMS

You should consider the first point before you begin to write any lengthy answer. You must try to grasp what the writer had set out to do. In other words, was Shakespeare simply filling up three hours of stage time with *Julius Caesar*? The plot could be summarised in a few pages, so why does the play take three hours on stage?

EXAMINER'S SECRET

There is no need to write reams; two to three sides of the answer book are enough to get up marks!

You might want to consider areas such as social comment. It is possible that Shakespeare was interested in raising issues such as the effects of power. Caesar wants absolute power and it turns out to be his downfall. Shakespeare is asking the audience to consider what the effect of such power might be. Brutus clearly feels that he knows no man could manage such limitless authority.

There were many playwrights of Shakespeare's day whose work is no longer performed so perhaps Shakespeare was doing something a little different to his fellow writers. The plot of *Julius Caesar* is quite complicated but it is the way that Shakespeare handles the various elements of plot that makes the play interesting. Look at the way that one part of the plot is built up to the point where a major event is about to take place and then the scene shifts to another area of plot altogether. An example would be both the soothsayer and Artemidorus trying to warn Caesar at the start of Act III Scene 1. This control of tension – making the audience wait – is a major element of Shakespeare's craft.

Remember: Shakespeare was a professional writer and he needed to please his audience.

MEANS

EXAMINER'S SECRET

If you are asked to compare something, this means showing the differences and the similarities.

Many students concentrate on the second point only: how did the writer write the piece? This results in a lengthy retelling of the story of whatever it is they have just read. There is nothing wrong with some account of the story but if this is all you do then you have carried out a fairly basic task. The plot of most great novels, plays and poems could be given to a class of eight-year-olds. They would then retell the story and draw a lovely picture. The skills shown by the eight year old students would not amount to much.

Remember: simply retelling the story is not a high level skill.

SUCCESS

When you do come to discuss the way that the writer went about achieving his/her aims there are some basic things that you need to do:

- Decide what it is you want to say
- Select the parts of the text that support what you want to say (see **How to use quotations**)

All too often students make sweeping statements without backing them up. Try to make you comments precise and to keep them in focus with regard to the question you are answering. A question on the effects of power in *Julius Caesar* does not require a discussion of every scene in the play. Good students know how to be selective.

Finish early to check through what you have written.

To reach the highest level you need to consider whether the writer has been successful. If you think Shakespeare set out to create a believable character in Antony, has he managed this? Do you think Shakespeare intended us to feel some sympathy for Cassius and, if so, has he made us feel it?

This area of your answer should reflect what you identified at the start, regarding what the writer set out to do. If a horror film is not frightening then it is not successful: think in this way about the play. You need to consider whether *Julius Caesar* works as a drama.

A higher-level answer will always contain the personal response of the student. Do not be afraid to say **'I feel that ...'** or **'I believe...'**. You must of course have some evidence for what you suggest. There are people who still think the Earth is flat but there is pretty good evidence that it is not.

Each time you make a major point you should support it, either by giving an account in your own words or by using a quotation.

Read through what you have written. If you have forgotten to put in paragraphs, the examiner will understand if you wirte 'NP' in the margin.

Two major elements of language which tend to be seen by only the best students are imagery and wit.

- You need to show how the use of imagery is responsible for creating particular impressions. For example, in Act I, Scene 3, line 25 Casca gives an account of the strange things that he has seen in the street: 'Men, all in fire, walk up and down the streets'. Such unusual events are designed to tell the audience that the heavens are disturbed by the events on earth.
- Writers know these associations and play upon them for effect. Take the simplest idea of all – villain dressed in black; good person dressed in white. Such basic images occur throughout the history of world literature. Good writers do not simply use such basic images. They are constantly looking out for new things to use as comparisons. You need to recognise that this is how writers work and include references to it in your written answers.
- Wit is a very big part of conversation in Shakespeare's plays. We would call wit 'intelligence'. Brutus believes that he has a greater wit than Antony, but we see at Caesar's funeral, that Brutus has badly misjudged Antony.

Everything you write is marked, even what you have crossed out. You may accidentally have crossed out something worth extra marks.

The final point to bear in mind is that your own writing needs to be of a high standard. You must attempt to use the language of literary criticism when discussing a work of literature. Simply saying **'the play was good'** does not really mean anything. It does not matter whether you liked the play; the important thing to remember is that you are commenting on the effectiveness of the work. Using vocabulary beyond that you might normally use when talking to your friends is vital if you wish to come across well on paper.

Don't forget the things you need to cover:

- AIMS: What did the writer set out to do?
- MEANS: How did the writer go about doing it?
- SUCCESS: Was the writer successful?

Good luck with your writing about Shakespeare.

SAMPLE ESSAY PLAN

A typical essay question on *Julius Caesar* is followed by a sample essay plan in note form. This does not present the only answer to the question, merely one answer. Do not be afraid to include your own ideas and leave out some of the ones in this sample! Remember that quotations are essential to prove and illustrate the points you make.

Say how far you think Caesar contributes to his own downfall.

The essay needs an introduction, main argument and conclusion. It is better to take a balanced view than to launch into a one-sided answer. The argument might be set out as follows.

Careful planning can save you time when writing and ensure that you do not lapse into storytelling.

Introduction

Refer to the definition of **tragedy** as a fall from greatness due to a flaw in character. If this is the case for Caesar he must have a flaw. In fact there are two major flaws in Caesar's nature: his ambition and his vanity, but he has strengths too.

Part 1

Discuss the strengths of Caesar. He has many strengths. One of the most important is his sense of public duty. Caesar treats the citizens well, as can be seen by their reaction in the opening scene. We see Caesar's human side at his first entrance: he wants Antony to touch Calpurnia in the race so that she might conceive a child. We see his strength of will when he dismisses the soothsayer as 'a dreamer' (I.2.24).

Caesar shows that he can be a good judge of character when he makes comments about Cassius. He also seems sure that Antony is loyal and trusts him enough to ask him to touch Calpurnia in the Lupercalia race. This shows that Caesar has faith in Antony (but also that he is desperate for an heir).

At the games Caesar's shameless manipulation of the crowd shows how shrewd he is. He knows what the people want to see and how to provide it.

We do not see Caesar the soldier in the play but his reputation as both a great general and a great fighter is referred to on several occasions.

Shakespeare may well have made Caesar seem vain and foolish in order to make the actions of Brutus seem noble.

On the way to the Capitol Caesar is stopped by Artemidorus. He shows another side here when refusing to read the petition of Artemidorus. He is told the petition concerns himself and so he says he will read it last. (**Ironically**, this public humility, whether real or sham, helps bring about his death.) There are signs here of the Caesar who was loved by the ordinary people of Rome.

Part 2

Now turn to the weaknesses of Caesar. Casca reports that Caesar could hardly bring himself to refuse the crown when it was offered to him at the games. There are clear signs here of the ambition of Caesar: he is not going to refuse the crown if it is offered to him again.

When Caesar next appears we see some signs of his vanity. He says his name is not 'liable to fear' (I.2.199). He then refers to himself as 'Caesar' for the first time. This might indicate foolish pride. Certainly he feels he is invulnerable.

Calpurnia succeeds in dissuading Caesar from going to the Capitol. It is his ambition and vanity which overcome his reason when Decius says that Calpurnia's dream is a good sign and that people will laugh at Caesar for doing what his wife tells him.

Caesar relaxes when surrounded by the conspirators and could be said to be either too trusting or too convinced that no one would dare to attack him to take precautions.

Conclusion

Caesar's ambition and vanity certainly contribute to his downfall. So too does his sense of public duty. This contradiction makes the character of Caesar and the play fascinating. There are certainly flaws in the character of Caesar and so the traditions of tragedy are observed.

FURTHER QUESTIONS

Make a plan as shown above and attempt these questions.

1. In what ways could *Julius Caesar* be said to be a great statesman?
2. On three separate occasions Brutus ignores advice from Cassius. Say what these occasions are and:
   a) Why Brutus ignores the advice and
   b) What the consequences are
3. Julius Caesar dies less than halfway through the play. Explain how Shakespeare maintains the audience's interest once Caesar is dead.
4. Brutus is a man torn between personal loyalty and public duty. Discuss the dilemma he faces over the murder of Caesar and say why you think he arrives at the decision he does.
5. Say how Shakespeare deals with power in *Julius Caesar*.
6. Discuss the portrayal of the relationship between
   a) Caesar and Calpurnia
   b) Brutus and Portia

   and show how far each man is influenced by his wife.
7. Discuss the character of Cassius and say how far your opinion of him has changed by the end of the play.
8. The supernatural plays an important part in *Julius Caesar*. Discuss the different ways in which the supernatural features in the play.
9. Is it inevitable that Brutus and Cassius die for their parts in the murder of Caesar?
10. Discuss Shakespeare's portrayal of Antony. Make particular reference to the funeral orations.

Remember to say how literary techniques are used – do not simply repeat them because you think they sound clever.

LITERARY TERMS

aside words spoken by a character in a play which some (or all) of the other characters on stage do not hear. Asides are often addressed directly to the audience and indicate the character's thoughts and feelings

blank verse lines which have rhythm or metre, but do not rhyme. Most of this play is in blank verse, with iambic pentameter as the type of verse used

construct an invention of the writer, crafted for a purpose

dramatic irony when the audience knows more about events in the play than the characters concerned, or what will happen as a result of one of the character's actions, for example, when Caesar unsuspectingly tells Trebonius (one of the conspirators) to draw close just before the assassins strike

figure of speech describing something in a more vivid or colourful way than is strictly necessary

heroic couplet two lines of iambic pentameter that rhyme. Shakespeare often uses an heroic couplet to mark the end of a scene (there were no stage curtains in the Elizabethan theatre) or to announce something very important

hyperbole deliberate exaggeration designed to achieve a particular effect

iambic pentameter a form of poetry in which the lines consist of five pairs of syllables, the first syllable is unstressed and is followed by one that is stressed; most of the speeches in this play are in iambic pentameter

imagery word pictures which help the audience (or reader) understand or interpret different events, for example, Brutus's description of his army's standards before the battle

irony/ironic saying (or writing) one thing, but meaning another, usually the opposite of what has been said

metre another word for rhythm; although there are many different types of rhythm, each one is simply a different arrangement of stressed and unstressed syllables

oration a formal speech made at a solemn public occasion, such as a funeral

pathos a quality which evokes feelings of pity and sorrow in the audience

prose what we would call 'ordinary speech', prose has no set pattern of rhythm. Characters speak in prose in Shakespeare's plays either because the person speaking is unimportant or the conversation is between people who know each other well and feel relaxed together. Prose is much less formal than verse. Compare the funeral oration given by Brutus, which is in prose, and Antony's which is in blank verse

pun a play on words; using a word that has two very different meanings. The Elizabethans were very fond of puns and considered that someone who could pun well was intelligent

rhetoric the art of speaking effectively and persuading an audience to accept your point of view, as Antony persuaded the people of Rome to turn against Caesar's murderers

rhyming couplet adjacent lines of any verse form which rhyme

soliloquy a speech made by a character directly to the audience which reveals his or her thoughts

tragedy a drama which traces the career and downfall of one of the characters due to a flaw in his or her character; Brutus says that ambition is Caesar's fatal flaw. In a tragedy the tragic hero or heroine brings about his or her own downfall

Checkpoint hints/answers

Checkpoint 1 Caesar has not achieved so much as his predecessor.

Checkpoint 2 It gives Caesar a chance to escape and so adds tension to the moment.

Checkpoint 3 Brutus loves Caesar but does not want him to become king.

Checkpoint 4 Cassius clearly hates Caesar.

Checkpoint 5 Signs of opposition to Caesar are suppressed.

Checkpoint 6 The natural order of the world seems disturbed.

Checkpoint 7 The messages will appear to have come from ordinary Romans.

Checkpoint 8 They are unsure of Brutus becuase of his close friendship with Caesar.

Checkpoint 9 This lets the audience know the assassination is near.

Checkpoint 10 Cassius fears that Mark Antony might seek revenge for Caesar's death.

Checkpoint 11 Decius knows that vanity is Caesar's weakness.

Checkpoint 12 Metellus's appeal is the signal to attack.

Checkpoint 13 Antony calls Caesar 'Julius', a sign of friendship.

Checkpoint 14 This is the sign for mass plunder and slaughter.

Checkpoint 15 Brutus is recognised as a great public figure.

Checkpoint 16 Antony deliberately makes Brutus appear dishonourable.

Checkpoint 17 Antony has already stirred the crowd with his speech.

Checkpoint 18 The people have been stirred by the words of Antony and have lost control of their actions.

Checkpoint 19 Antony proves himself to be a shrewd judge of men, though a harsh one.

Checkpoint 20 Brutus points out that Cassius did not confront Caesar but plotted behind his back.

Checkpoint 21 Eagles catch and kill their own prey; ravens, crows and kites eat carrion, feeding off human corpses and other dead things.

Checkpoint 22 The eagle was an important symbol of power in Ancient Rome and was part of the standard of each legion.

Checkpoint 23 Each man dies on the sword that helped kill Caesar.

Checkpoint 24 Brutus is indeed a noble Roman.

Checkpoint 25 Each day is roughly an hour long.

Test answers

Test yourself (Act I)

1 Caesar (*Scene 2*)

2 Brutus (*Scene 2*)

3 Cassius (*Scene 2*)

4 Brutus (*Scene 2*)

5 Casca (*Scene 3*)

6 Caesar (*Scene 2*)

7 Cassius (*Scene 2*)

8 Brutus (*Scene 2*)

Test yourself (Act II)

1 Brutus (*Scene 1*)

2 Cassius (*Scene 1*)

3 Calpurnia (*Scene 2*)

4 Portia (*Scene 4*)

5 Artemidorus (*Scene 3*)

6 Caesar (*Scene 1*)

7 Cicero (*Scene 1*)

8 Caesar (*Scene 2*)

Test yourself (Act III)

1 Popillius (*Scene 1*)

2 Cinna (*Scene 1*)

3 Antony (*Scene 1*)

4 Brutus (*Scene 2*)

5 Antony (*Scene 2*)

6 Metellus (*Scene 1*)

7 Brutus (*Scene 1*)

8 The people of Rome (*Scene 2*)

Test yourself (Act IV)

1 Octavius (*Scene 1*)

2 Brutus (*Scene 2*)

3 Cassius (*Scene 3*)

4 Messala (*Scene 3*)

5 Caesar's ghost (*Scene 3*)

6 Lepidus (*Scene 1*)

7 Cassius (*Scene 3*)

Test yourself (Act V)

1 Brutus (*Scene 1*)

2 Brutus (*Scene 1*)

3 Titinius (*Scene 3*)

4 Octavius (*Scene 5*)

5 Antony (*Scene 5*)

6 Brutus, Cassius and the conspirators (*Scene 1*)

7 Cassius (*Scene 3*)

8 Brutus (*Scene 5*)

NOTES

Notes

York Notes for GCSE

Maya Angelou
I Know Why the Caged Bird Sings

Jane Austen
Pride and Prejudice

Alan Ayckbourn
Absent Friends

Elizabeth Barrett Browning
Selected Poems

Robert Bolt
A Man for All Seasons

Harold Brighouse
Hobson's Choice

Charlotte Brontë
Jane Eyre

Emily Brontë
Wuthering Heights

Shelagh Delaney
A Taste of Honey

Charles Dickens
David Copperfield
Great Expectations
Hard Times
Oliver Twist

Roddy Doyle
Paddy Clarke Ha Ha Ha

George Eliot
Silas Marner
The Mill on the Floss

Anne Frank
The Diary of a Young Girl

William Golding
Lord of the Flies

Oliver Goldsmith
She Stoops to Conquer

Willis Hall
The Long and the Short and the Tall

Thomas Hardy
Far from the Madding Crowd
The Mayor of Casterbridge
Tess of the d'Urbervilles
The Withered Arm and other Wessex Tales

L.P. Hartley
The Go-Between

Seamus Heaney
Selected Poems

Susan Hill
I'm the King of the Castle

Barry Hines
A Kestrel for a Knave

Louise Lawrence
Children of the Dust

Harper Lee
To Kill a Mockingbird

Laurie Lee
Cider with Rosie

Arthur Miller
The Crucible
A View from the Bridge

Robert O'Brien
Z for Zachariah

Frank O'Connor
My Oedipus Complex and Other Stories

George Orwell
Animal Farm

J.B. Priestley
An Inspector Calls
When We Are Married

Willy Russell
Educating Rita
Our Day Out

J.D. Salinger
The Catcher in the Rye

William Shakespeare
Henry IV Part I
Henry V
Julius Caesar
Macbeth
The Merchant of Venice
A Midsummer Night's Dream
Much Ado About Nothing
Romeo and Juliet
The Tempest
Twelfth Night

George Bernard Shaw
Pygmalion

Mary Shelley
Frankenstein

R.C. Sherriff
Journey's End

Rukshana Smith
Salt on the snow

John Steinbeck
Of Mice and Men

Robert Louis Stevenson
Dr Jekyll and Mr Hyde

Jonathan Swift
Gulliver's Travels

Robert Swindells
Daz 4 Zoe

Mildred D. Taylor
Roll of Thunder, Hear My Cry

Mark Twain
Huckleberry Finn

James Watson
Talking in Whispers

Edith Wharton
Ethan Frome

William Wordsworth
Selected Poems

A Choice of Poets

Mystery Stories of the Nineteenth Century including The Signalman

Nineteenth Century Short Stories

Poetry of the First World War

Six Women Poets

York Notes advanced

Margaret Atwood
Cat's Eye
The Handmaid's Tale

Jane Austen
Emma
Mansfield Park
Persuasion
Pride and Prejudice
Sense and Sensibility

Alan Bennett
Talking Heads

William Blake
Songs of Innocence and of Experience

Charlotte Brontë
Jane Eyre
Villette

Emily Brontë
Wuthering Heights

Angela Carter
Nights at the Circus

Geoffrey Chaucer
The Franklin's Prologue and Tale
The Miller's Prologue and Tale
The Prologue to the Canterbury Tales
The Wife of Bath's Prologue and Tale

Samuel Coleridge
Selected Poems

Joseph Conrad
Heart of Darkness

Daniel Defoe
Moll Flanders

Charles Dickens
Bleak House
Great Expectations
Hard Times

Emily Dickinson
Selected Poems

John Donne
Selected Poems

Carol Ann Duffy
Selected Poems

George Eliot
Middlemarch
The Mill on the Floss

T.S. Eliot
Selected Poems
The Waste Land

F. Scott Fitzgerald
The Great Gatsby

E.M. Forster
A Passage to India

Brian Friel
Translations

Thomas Hardy
Jude the Obscure
The Mayor of Casterbridge
The Return of the Native
Selected Poems
Tess of the d'Urbervilles

Seamus Heaney
Selected Poems from 'Opened Ground'

Nathaniel Hawthorne
The Scarlet Letter

Homer
The Iliad
The Odyssey

Aldous Huxley
Brave New World

Kazuo Ishiguro
The Remains of the Day

Ben Jonson
The Alchemist

James Joyce
Dubliners

John Keats
Selected Poems

Christopher Marlowe
Doctor Faustus
Edward II

Arthur Miller
Death of a Salesman

John Milton
Paradise Lost Books I & II

Toni Morrison
Beloved

George Orwell
Nineteen Eighty-Four

Sylvia Plath
Selected Poems

Alexander Pope
Rape of the Lock & Selected Poems

William Shakespeare
Antony and Cleopatra
As You Like It
Hamlet
Henry IV Part I
King Lear
Macbeth
Measure for Measure
The Merchant of Venice
A Midsummer Night's Dream
Much Ado About Nothing
Othello
Richard II
Richard III
Romeo and Juliet
The Taming of the Shrew
The Tempest
Twelfth Night
The Winter's Tale

George Bernard Shaw
Saint Joan

Mary Shelley
Frankenstein

Jonathan Swift
Gulliver's Travels and A Modest Proposal

Alfred Tennyson
Selected Poems

Virgil
The Aeneid

Alice Walker
The Color Purple

Oscar Wilde
The Importance of Being Earnest

Tennessee Williams
A Streetcar Named Desire

Jeanette Winterson
Oranges Are Not the Only Fruit

John Webster
The Duchess of Malfi

Virginia Woolf
To the Lighthouse

W.B. Yeats
Selected Poems

Metaphysical Poets